DAVID WILD

MAIN
STREET
BOOKS

DOUBLEDAY New York London Toronto Sydney Auckland

F·R·I·E·N·D·S

The Official Companion

A Main Street Book

PUBLISHED BY DOUBLEDAY

a division of Bantam Doubleday Dell Publishing Group, Inc.

1540 Broadway, New York, New York 10036

Main Street Books, Doubleday, and the portrayal of a building

with a tree are trademarks of Doubleday, a division of

Bantam Doubleday Dell Publishing Group, Inc.

Designed by Bonni Leon-Berman

Library of Congress Cataloging-in-Publication Data

  Wild, David, 1961–
  Friends : the official companion / David Wild. — 1st ed.
      p.   cm.
  "A Main Street book"—Verso t.p.
  1. Friends (Television program)—Miscellanea.
PN1992.77.F76W56   1995
791.45'72—dc20   95-39077
                                        CIP

ISBN 0-385-48329-5

TM and copyright ©1995 by Warner Bros.

Printed in the United States of America

December 1995

10 9 8 7 6 5 4 3 2 1

First Edition

Acknowledgments

Thanks are due to all the friendly folks at *Friends*, including Kevin S. Bright, Marta Kauffman, and David Crane, the show's cast, and Todd Stevens, as well as Warner Bros. Worldwide Publishing's Grace Ressler and advertising and publicity executive Barbara Brogliatti, and Phil Gonzales.

I am especially indebted to Bruce Tracy, my editor at Doubleday, for his amazing grace under pressure, and to Melanie Jackson, my tough but fair agent.

Thanks also go out to everyone at *Rolling Stone,* particularly Tom Conroy, who edited my cover story on *Friends*; and Kristina Wells, who contributed research.

As always, I'm most grateful for the loving support of my entire family, my own friends, and especially Fran, my wife and best friend.

Contents

FRIENDS DEAREST

**One Monkey's Totally Uncensored Tail-All
About the Scandalous and Sometimes
Downright Unfriendly Behavior
Behind the Scenes at America's Favorite TV Show**

When my close personal friend and total pit bull of an agent Sol Bananberg of the William Morris Agency first informed me about a moderately generous book offer to pen my memoirs early this spring, I quickly and politely declined. Over brunch at Jerry's Famous Deli in Studio City, I kibitzed with Sol regarding my serious reservations about committing to such a project. After all, I'm a monkey still in my twenties, and believe me, bubby, this particular tale ain't over yet. Even with all my extraordinary recent success—my seminal work in *Friends* and *Outbreak*, as well as an upcoming infomercial and what I believe will be a ground-breaking CD-ROM/exercise video package that's currently in preproduction—I figured I was far too busy *doing* to waste any time blowing my own horn to some less-evolved ghost writer.

"What's the *rush?*" I wondered aloud over a delicious platter of bagels, nova, and plantains. Humbly, I figured that I'd get around to telling my whole remarkable and moving life story later when I was done living it. As the saying goes, "Monkey see, monkey do until all the gigs all dry up, and *then* monkey write," right? Furthermore, being a serious-minded, literary kinda beast by nature, I didn't want to waste my time writing just another typically animalistic celebrity memoir about my life in this crazy zoo that I so fondly call "the business of show." Call me pretentious, but I didn't want to see my good name emblazoned on some trade paperback unless it was an important book of real substance, something weighty like Charles Darwin's *Origin of Species*, George Orwell's *Animal Farm*, Kurt Vonnegut's *Welcome to the Monkey House*, or that woefully underappreciated novelization of *Every Which Way but Loose*.

So I passed.

Now cut to just a few action-packed months later. Fortunately for you, the mammal reader, I found myself having what can only be called a profound change of heart. In May, of course, I made national headlines when I left *Friends* under famously difficult and tense circumstances after I was falsely accused of eating the scenery. Of course, my departure might have gotten a whole hell of a lot more media play if Julia Roberts and Lyle Lovett hadn't picked the exact same goddamn day to announce *their* split. Guess what monkey's publicist was canned the very next morning? Then a few weeks later, summer repeats began, and *Friends* started hitting the number one spot in the weekly Nielsens as a matter of course. Seemingly overnight, my cute little show had grown into a full-blown, friggin' phenomenon.

And so before long, the fine folks at Doubleday ran some numbers again, upped the ante considerably, and gave in on some crucial issues regarding ancillary rights. By an incredibly fortuitous coincidence, it was at that exact moment that a grand realization struck me: As hard as I tried to deny it, the truth was that I had a responsibility, a *calling*, if you will, to set the record straight and tell the truth about the show so many call *Friends*.

The people have a right to know, I realized, and as the last honest monkey in Tinseltown, damn it, *I* was going to have to be the one to tell them. After all—as we say on a high holiday that eludes me at the moment—if not me, then *who*? If not now, then *when*? Sure, a fully sanitized version of events regarding *Friends* may emerge elsewhere, but by virtue of a little luck and a whole lot of God-given talent, I alone was an honest witness to the true story of America's most beloved TV sitcom.

Sadly, there were many vicious and damaging untruths spread by a barbaric media, the worst being that infamous May 1995 *Rolling Stone* cover story by one David Wild, a gutless punk who misquoted me extensively despite not having had the decency to even call my people to schedule an official interview. Furthermore, despite Mr. Wild's "article," I *never* demanded that the show's title be changed to *Marcel's Friends*. I simply pointed out to NBC President Warren Littlefield that my brethren on *Me and the Chimp* and *Lancelot Link, Secret Chimp* got much, *much* better billing than I did.

Shortly after that vindictive piece of gutter journalism hit the newsstands, I left the gilded cage of *Friends* under less than ideal circumstances. Suddenly I was free to do what thousands of great Americans and approximately a half-dozen Simpson jurors have done before me: tell my side of a hot story for fun, for profit, and, most important, for *you*, the American people.

For the record, let me make this next fact perfectly clear: Before I flew to New York and signed the final contract for this book you hold in your hot little paws, I put in calls to the show's Executive Producers Marta Kauffman, David Crane, and Kevin Bright, Producer Todd Stevens, and each and every one of my former costars, Courteney Cox, Jennifer Aniston, Lisa Kudrow, Matthew Perry, and Matt LeBlanc. I even phoned the individual who was both my closest colleague and (I don't think I'm spilling any coffee beans here) my most unfriendly adversary, a man I call David Schwimmer.

I should explain that I made these difficult calls less because I was advised by legal counsel to do so than because I felt that, ultimately, it was quite simply the *right* thing to do. Too often, those of us who toil within the Hollywood dream factory let all the middlemen and -women—the talent agents, the managers, the lawyers, the spin doctors, the animal trainers— get in the way of just talking these matters out one on one. Hell, if William Shatner, a big talent who, incidentally, I'd *love* to work with, was big enough to call up all the folks on *Star Trek* who couldn't stand him for his book, then I could certainly get on the cellular with some ex-friends for mine. If Barry Williams can get all familial one more time with the now balding Brady Bunch, then I sure as hell can get on the honker and be awfully friendly for literature's sake.

Remember how it took a lot of years (and *Frank Sinatra*, for God's sake) to finally get Dean Martin and Jerry Lewis back together? Initially I had hoped that for David and me all it would take was one book deal with an unusually generous royalty rate for the healing to begin. And while, sadly, a pending restraining order made it inadvisable for me and my old pals to meet within fifty yards of one another, we all talked our hearts out in a series of frank, emotional, intimate, revealing, and, most important, audiotaped phone conversations.

Had I not made this extra effort, this book would be little more than one monkey's star trip, a sort of *How to Star in* Friends *and Influence People*. But that just wasn't good enough for me, or for the folks who control the purse strings at Doubleday. And so, what follows is, in a very real sense, not only *my* story, but also *our* story of *Friends*—except, of course, I'm the only one who gets paid.

I'd love to take total personal credit for making *Friends*— and, indeed, I did exactly that in my initial draft of this text before it was vetted by the publisher's attorneys. But from a strict legal point of view, I have to give much of the credit to Marta Kauffman, Kevin S. Bright, and David Crane.

Kauffman and Crane have been friends and creative partners since their days studying at Brandeis University in Waltham, Massachusetts, an excellent school despite a history of shamefully low simian attendance and a spotty record in the treatment of exotic animals in general. After graduation, the two Philadelphia natives moved on to the Big Apple and made a splash in the theater world with the Off-Broadway musicals *A . . . My Name Is Alice* and *Personals*.

The New York–born Kevin S. Bright, son of vaudeville comedian Jackie Bright, attended Emerson College in Boston. He went on to work in New York, producing variety specials for everyone from George Burns to David Copperfield. Moving to Los Angeles, he became an Emmy and Ace award–winning producer of numerous comedy specials that found him working with Robin Williams, Martin Mull, and Harry Shearer, among many others, as well as serving as supervising producer of *In Living Color* and executive producer of *The Ron Reagan Show* (a show hosted by the son of Ronald Reagan, fondly recalled for his work in that film classic *Bedtime for Bonzo*).

In 1990 Kauffman and Crane broke into TV in high style by creating the highly influential and popular HBO comedy series *Dream On*. It was while working on the *Dream On* pilot in the fall of 1989 that they met Kevin Bright. The partnership among these three executive producers would blossom over three seasons of high wit, inspired comedy, and the occasional tit shot. Too much monkey business? I think not. Right from the beginning, *Dream On* was smart, adult, funny, funny stuff. Less successful were two other efforts at series: *The Powers That Be*, which was created by Kauffman and Crane for Norman Lear and ran for one season on NBC, and *Family Album*, which heartbreakingly lasted only six episodes on CBS in 1993.

After dusting themselves off from these experiences, our holy triumvirate—encouraged by the support of then Warner Brothers Television President Leslie Moonves—got busy and started pitching three new sitcoms to the networks for the fall of 1994. One of those ideas was for a TV musical series. Having read for a recurring role on *Cop Rock* myself, a few seasons back, even *I* knew that baby wouldn't sell.

NBC eventually did sign on for a show called *Friends Like Us*, which would tell the story of six people in their twenties and their lives together in New York City. Inexplicably, my character was not envisioned as part of the original ensemble. Soon enough, it would become painfully obvious to every TV-watching, fur-bearing creature that something—or someone—was missing.

"A year before the pilot, we started talking about doing a show about people in their twenties, just because it's such a great group to write about," Marta told me. "It's such an exciting time in your life, and such a confusing time, too."

When Sol first messengered over the pilot script to my pad, I must confess that I made the mistake others would make—I figured *Friends* looked like some contrived *Reality Bites: The Show*. "A bunch of good-looking white kids hanging around drinking fancy coffee in New York" as I was misquoted as saying in *Rolling Stone*. Well, hold the presses, the fact is that I was dead wrong. "This show had nothing to do with market testing something to Generation X," Marta told me.

The executive producers say that while they did talk to people in their twenties early on for the sake of research, they ended up mostly using their own experiences of living in New York when they were in their twenties. "Obviously, we're not all that different," Marta added.

The truth of the matter may be that the comedy of *Friends* is actually pretty timeless stuff. "We figured out pretty early on that *Friends* is really just about very universal emotional situations," David Crane said. "It's about falling in love, finding a job, dealing with parents, death, birth, monkeys, and lesbians." (Thanks for the billing there, Dave.)

First, there was the matter of finding the actors and actresses to bring this new show to life. Working with casting director Ellie Kanner, the executives went to work casting the roles of Monica Geller, Rachel Green, Phoebe Buffay, Ross Geller, Chandler Bing, and Joey Tribbiani in the spring of 1994. A little-known fact—and one that may help explain some tensions that would emerge later—is that I too read for both the Ross and Joey roles.

As I've long contended, I'm simply too good an actor and too much of a professional to confine myself to roles specifically written for my species.

How else is a formally trained primate ever going to show his range? Unfortunately, I got the clear sense that I was never seriously considered for either role. Officially, the reason passed on to Sol for my not getting a callback was that it was strictly "a height issue." Hey, I may look like a chimp, but don't forget I ain't *nobody's* chump.

Kauffman calculated that she, David, and Kevin saw a "gazillion" actors read for each *Friends* role, though more dependable sources put the figure slightly lower at seventy-five. After this rather exhausting cattle call—a phrase that, I must admit, has never been a favorite of mine—the cast for the *Friends* pilot finally came together.

First let's discuss the fine women of *Friends*—the show's *real* Central Perks, in my personal opinion.

The fussy but lovable Monica—a babe with seemingly inexplicable boy trouble—would be played by Courteney Cox. Cox was *Friends'* most familiar face initially, and what a pretty face at that. Before I go any further, let me take this opportunity to clear up an all too common misconception: Despite all the innuendo and gossip, Courteney and I were *never* more than friends. Though we always shared a very special and spiritual connection, as well as a passion for candy and junk food, the truth is that during my entire tenure at *Friends* I was in a committed relationship with Dotty, a gifted and gorgeous makeup woman whose acquaintance I'd made while shooting *Outbreak*.

Like so many others, I first spotted Courteney back in 1984 as the adorably wholesome-looking girl whom Bruce Springsteen pulls up onstage in the Brian De Palma-directed video for "Dancing in the Dark." Now I love "Court," but I gotta admit I go a little ape when I ponder the fact that she was working with the Boss and De Palma right out of the gate. No crappy dinner theater or poorly paying wildlife park gigs for Ms. Cox. "Someone once told me that I'm only in the video for twenty-four seconds," said Courteney. "But I got a lot of recognition out of those seconds. After that, I lived in New York and people would want me to tell them what's he *really* like? Are you Bruce's sister? Are you his girlfriend? Who *are* you?"

The Birmingham, Alabama, native and former model went on to numerous TV roles, most notably playing Lauren, the girlfriend of Alex P. Keaton (Michael J. Fox), on *Family Ties* from 1986 to 1988. The supreme "Court" also appeared in a number of movies, including *Cocoon: The Return*, *Masters of the Universe*, and, most successfully, *Ace Ventura: Pet Detective*, which found her starring with an extraordinary cast of creatures (as well as that crazy kid Jim Carrey).

Right before getting the *Friends* gig, Cox starred in the short-lived series *The Trouble with Larry*, alongside Bronson Pinchot. The diplomatic Ms. Cox understates things when she jokes "there was *lots* of trouble with *Larry*." Still, thespian to thespian, Courteney confided in me that she was actually grateful that she did *Larry*. "I had fun; I

LEAN CUISINE: The lithe Monica cooks up something in the pilot episode

got to play very sarcastic and dry," Courteney offered. "That show also kind of led to this job since they were both for Warner Bros. It worked out great in the end."

Originally, the trio of *Friends'* executive producers saw Courteney as possibly being the right woman to play a different role. "They said, 'We see you more as Rachel,'" Court remembered. "But I would have played Rachel as much more neurotic and I wouldn't have been as good as Jennifer is. See, I'm not a quirky person, although I'd like to be. I think it looks fun to be quirky, but I just don't have it in me. I'm working toward being a kook."

Don't worry, babe, in this business, you'll get there soon enough.

"We always figured Courteney was a Rachel because she's so pretty," David Crane recalled. "And she kept saying, 'No, no, no, I'm Monica.' She insisted on reading, and then she just knocked us out because she was so funny—we'd never had a chance to see her be this funny before."

The pretty woman and funny lady who finally was cast as Rachel was, of course, Jennifer Aniston, whom the executive producers had originally seen as a Monica. "We didn't see a Rachel at all until Jennifer walked in," said Marta. "Then it was amazing because there Rachel was. Jennifer just had this incredible ability to play such a brat and make you love her anyway."

Let me take this opportunity to clear up another common misconception: Despite all the innuendo and gossip, Jennifer and I were nothing more than friends. Though we always shared a special connection—we both grew up in this crazy business—the truth is that during my entire tenure at *Friends* I was in a committed relationship with Dotty, a gifted, gorgeous, and spiri-

PRINCESS OF THE WEST VILLAGE: A newly fiancé-less and credit card-less Rachel in the pilot episode

tual makeup woman whose acquaintance I'd made while shooting *Outbreak*.

Despite growing up a real show biz kid, "Jen" Aniston is truly a living doll. Her dad, John Aniston, has starred for years on the soap *Days of Our Lives*, and her godfather was the late Telly Savalas, of *Kojak* fame. And though she was not encouraged by her family to go into acting, Jen got in anyway, and got in young. From her formative roles as a rock and a thorn in school plays, she went on to attend New York City's High School for the Performing Arts, better known to those of us in the trade as the *Fame* school. "There was no dancing on taxicabs or the cafeteria tables," Jen explained, "but it was an amazing experience."

After graduating in 1987, Jennifer did some excellent stage work in the city (I say this as a proud Strasberg disciple myself). Then she went west, where she joined the cast of the show *Molloy* before going on to appear in *Ferris Bueller, Herman's Head*, and the sketch comedy show *The Edge*. Aniston was also in the cast of the short-lived series *Muddling Through*, on which she found herself doing exactly that. And though she'd turn green if she knew I was telling you, she also did that woefully misunderstood 1993 Celtic slasher flick *Leprechaun*.

With Rachel Green, Jennifer finally found a character she could sink her teeth into. "Rachel's not your clichéd princess," she elaborated. "She's not stupid or flighty. She's just not had to think about a lot of things before. She's never had to support herself or worry about much of *any-thing* really."

It's with head in paws that I report that the tabloid accounts of Jennifer and I clashing openly during the taping of "The One Where the Monkey Gets Away" episode are, sadly, true. In good faith, I must take the monkey's share of the blame here. My only excuse is that I was dealing with some very raw material on the show, and I think I got a little "methody" on the set in my effort to break through that fourth wall. Sorry, funny lady.

There were never any problems between myself and Lisa Kudrow, a real classy babe who was selected early on to play *Friends'* space case Phoebe Buffay. But let me take this opportunity to clear up another common misconception: Despite all the innuendo and gossip, Lisa and I were nothing more than friends. Though we always shared what I like to think was a great mutual respect and a knack for improvisational comedy, the truth is that during my entire tenure at *Friends* I was in a committed relationship with Dotty, a gifted, gorgeous, and spiritual makeup woman whose acquaintance I'd made while shooting *Outbreak*. Message to Michel Stern, her new fortunate French ad man husband: Congratulations, Frenchy, the best *man* won.

THE ORIGINAL RIOT GRRRL: A busking Phoebe plays her heart out

"Lisa is just brilliantly funny and yet very real," David Crane gushed unapologetically. "In other hands, Phoebe could potentially be so tedious, obvious, and fake and broad, and somehow she makes all her moments so real. That her character—which is by far our broadest—could move you as often as she does is really remarkable."

Believe you me, this native Californian is no hippie ditz. "People who don't know me will sometimes talk to me very slowly so that I'll be able to follow them," Lisa recalled with a laugh. This lovely lady graduated from Vassar College with a degree in biology and began working with her father Dr. Lee Kudrow, a world-famous headache specialist, before detouring into comedy with the encouragement of Jon Lovitz, a friend of her older brother's.

By 1989 Kudrow was a member of the famed improvisational theater group The Groundlings, in Los Angeles. Before long, she was turning up with increasing regularity on shows like *Cheers, Coach*, and *Newhart*. Most famously, she was cast as *Mad About You*'s Ursula, America's best-loved bad waitress (at least until Rachel Green came along). Before that, though, Kudrow did catch a bad break when she was cast as Roz on *Frasier* and then quickly replaced. Personally, I'd consider this no blemish on Lisa's record, especially considering the painful overacting they allow that blasted Eddie the Dog to get away with on that otherwise charming show.

As for the gentlemen of *Friends*, my relationships with them were perhaps unavoidably much more problematic—clearly there was a sense of competition built into the gig.

Cast as the less than brainy Joey Tribbiani, Matt LeBlanc was probably the easiest of my fellow leading men to get along with and get to know. He's a sweet kid, and that quality comes through in his performance. "We never imagined that the character would have so much heart to him," confessed Kauffman. Crane was similarly charmed: "Matt made Joey a hunky guy, but he's also a benign, sweet presence that we *never* imagined."

After graduating from high school, LeBlanc went to New York City, and after flipping burgers for a period, it wasn't long before he began to make a living in commercials. By 1988 Matt—a real motorbike enthusiast—was studying acting and soon moved to Los Angeles and ended up on the series

TV 101. From there he won roles in the series *Top of the Heap* and *Vinnie & Bobbie* and in that saucy *Red Shoe Diaries*. In none of these roles did LeBlanc play a guy who you'd call a rocket scientist. Here's another basis for the unspoken but unbreakable connection between the two of us: Both of us know all too well the pain of being consistently asked to play dumb.

"That's been a weird situation," admitted LeBlanc. "If you do something well, people tend to want to give you those roles. Joey is sort of a dim guy, but he's not just a dumb guy. I'd hate to be stereotyped, but then again there are five hundred guys who would kill to be in my situation." Like we always used to remind each other, Matt, it's a jungle out here.

Meanwhile, the role of Chandler Bing, Joey's chronically wiseass roommate, went to Matthew Perry, whom I've referred to in the past as The Great Unknowable.

Professionally speaking, I have nothing but praise for the guy. As Marta told me, "Matthew's just so brilliant, he can make a joke work that would never work in anyone else's hands." According to David, "Sometimes the writers will sit around and try to guess what Matthew's going to do with a line and which words he'll emphasize. Still, he always surprises us."

What surprised me with Matthew Perry was my utter inability to *really* get to know him. When you're caught up inside the whirlwind of a smash show, there aren't too many outsiders who understand what you are going through. But I always got the impression Matthew would rather hang out with the equally hairy George Clooney next door at *ER* than with me, his own castmate. And while he gave me a lot of laughs with his own Chandleresque quips, I regret that the two of us never found the time to really talk until now.

In fact, it wasn't until our conversation for this book that I felt I *really* got to know Matthew as a man. Perry, who grew up in Ottawa, Canada, was a nationally ranked teen tennis player. His father is actor John Bennett Perry, who's perhaps best known as the oppressively manly sailor on all those Old Spice commercials. His mother, Suzanne Perry, is a former anchorwoman and a onetime aide to Canadian Prime Minister Pierre Trudeau. Matthew got his first role in seventh grade, playing the fastest gun in the West in a production called *The Death and Life of Sneaky Finch*. And though I've not personally seen the reviews, Matthew told me it was some of his bravest, most powerful work.

With credits like that, it's no surprise that when he moved to this loony City of Angels, Matty boy found no shortage of work. He made guest appearances on *Charles in Charge, Beverly Hills 90210,* and *Growing Pains.* "It's kind of a blur, but on *90210* I remember playing the most popular kid in school who ends up with a gun in his mouth because his dad's overbearing," he fondly recalled.

"Admiral" Perry also popped up in features like *A Night in the Life of Jimmy Reardon*, with River Phoenix, and *She's Out of Control*, which found him working with Ami Dolenz, the daughter of that distinguished former Monkee Micky Dolenz. Perry had a little less luck with his own series: He starred in Fox's *Second Chance*, which quickly turned into *Boys Will Be Boys*, which quickly became nothing at all. He also turned up opposite Valerie Bertinelli in the 1990 series *Sydney*, as well as on something called *Home Free*, which is not to be confused with the classic *Born Free*.

"If you look at my first stuff, there's some bad acting going on that would make me cringe now," confessed Matthew. "But I actually always had an attitude. I was ninety-second in the ratings with all this attitude."

I'm happy to say that after our soul-and-fur-bearing conversation, I have a whole new attitude about Matthew.

Dear reader, I only wish that the same could be said about my relationship, such as it is, with David Schwimmer, the enormously complicated and talented young man who was cast as the much put-upon Ross.

For the life of me, I cannot pinpoint exactly when things went so horribly wrong between us. All I know is that through his representatives Schwimmer passed along word that he would have "no comment." Sorry to bug you, Mister Big Stuff.

Still, I like to believe that our work together speaks for itself. Like Martin and Lewis, Simon and Garfunkel, and Sacco and Vanzetti, I think there was some indefinable but undeniable magic that happened when we met beneath the spotlights. Hopefully, episodes like "The One with the Monkey" and "The One Where the Monkey Gets Away" will outlive any bitterness either of us may feel.

That said, David is of course—even without me to play off—a fine and generous actor. He's the son of two lawyers and attended Beverly Hills High School, which might explain something since I'm clearly a guy who grew up in a zoo on the other side of the tracks.

As a teenager, David shined at the Southern California Shakespeare Festival, and played Otto Frank in *The Diary of Anne Frank*. Having attended a summer workshop in acting at Northwestern University in Chicago, he went on to earn his degree there in speech/theater in 1988. Afterward, he and some of his Northwestern pals formed the adventurous Lookingglass Theater Company, where he directed an award-winning production of one of my favorite works, *The Jungle*.

Soon, David was turning up on shows like *The Wonder Years, NYPD Blue*, and *L.A. Law*, and in movies such as *Wolf, Crossing the Bridge*, and *Twenty Bucks*. His debut as a TV-series regular on 1993's wobbly Henry Winkler vehicle *Monty* was a less than thrilling one. "The only thing that I learned was that I was not going to do another situation comedy," Schwimmer told the clod from *Rolling Stone*.

"We had to beg him to come back from Chicago since he was not that excited about doing another television show after *Monty*," Bright confided in me. Still, the executive producers felt that this long-distance Schwimmer was well worth pursuing.

"David doesn't have a false move in him," Marta said. "He's just so honest and real and funny."

"Of all the actors, he was the only one who was really in our heads when we wrote the role," Kevin Bright explained. "But even then, David surprised us with his abilities as a physical comedian."

Now, the production triumvirate had its original players.

"We found a dream cast," Marta said a tad wistfully. "If we can write it, they can do it."

Friends was becoming a show with everything . . . except for a single goddamn monkey.

Slowly but surely, *Friends* came together. Finding the right name itself took a little time. Along the way, your slacker-era show of shows was almost called *Insomnia Café, Six of One, Across the Hall*, and *Friends Like Us*.

Then NBC called the executive producers to say that they were going to put *Friends* on during its powerhouse Thursday lineup, a dream slot alongside *Seinfeld, Mad About You*, and another promising new show called *ER*. As we say in TV, there are three major rules—location, location, location. In that same conversation, the network asked the powers that be if they minded calling the show simply *Friends*. "You can call it *Kevorkian*," an elated Kevin Bright told NBC.

Also signing on were all sort of other talented behind-the-scene types like Producer Todd Stevens, the benevolent dictator whose job it is to crack the whip to get the show done, and the famed TV director James Burrows, the much-in-demand sitcom *auteur* who helmed the *Friends* pilot and three other episodes during the first season (including "The One with All the Poker," for which I just happened to get some of the finest notices of my career).

Then, of course, there are our fantastic writers—"our friendly neighborhood scribes" as I charmingly dubbed them. The old saw goes that if you put a thousand monkeys in front of a typewriter for a million years, eventually they'd produce a *Friends* script. Personally, I don't think it would take quite *that* long. But even though others have correctly pointed out that I never got my fair share of the dialogue, I would still stack the *Friends* wordsmiths against anyone else in the business.

"Writing for *Friends* is a very democratic process," explained Jeff Greenstein, a supervising producer during the first season who went on to cocreate Fox's *Partners* with writing partner Jeff Strauss. "Basically, it's a matter of the best joke wins."

"We have the sort of writers who would be there at two in the morning, and they would be writers fighting over commas," David Crane offered with justifiable pride.

Whatever our differences, I assured the executive producers that we always did offer our viewers the very best commas on network television.

"Thank you very much," replied Crane. "I'm particularly proud of our punctuation."

"We give great ellipses . . ." added Kauffman, before trailing off.

Of course, *someone* has to deliver the lines.

"We've also been lucky enough to have a group of actors who can add something to the writing and even bring in their own jokes," Kauffman noted. Matthew Perry in particular should carry a PowerBook with him at all times.

"I think we knew we had something special at the first run-through," David Crane told me. "You simply looked at them and you went, 'This could be *really* good.' All of a sudden, the whole thing wasn't so theoretical anymore."

As the first season progressed, the trio were pleasantly surprised to find things falling into place, albeit with insane amounts of hard work. "We had this thing on Tuesday nights, after taping the show, we'd usually say to one another, '*Wow*, another one that didn't suck,'" mused Kauffman.

They soon found that far from sucking, they were actually moving people. "One of the things on the Internet I read," Kauffman told me, "was somebody writing that they were watching the episode where Marcel's in the hospital, and he wrote 'I can't believe I'm watching some monkey squeeze a guy's finger and I'm welling up. Why is this happening?' " I believe it's called *acting*, you cyberpunk.

Yes, as some of my detractors have pointed out, it's true that I didn't join the *Friends* ensemble until the first season's tenth episode, "The One with the Monkey," which aired for the first time on December 15, 1994. But it can also be argued that it was exactly at this time that the show hit a real ratings bump and started emotionally connecting with its audience.

Screw that whole Ross/Rachel romantic tension, *I* know what brought the masses into the show. Let me put it this way: *All-American Girl, Pig Sty*, and *Slap Maxwell* all had no monkey and failed. *Friends*, *avec moi*, became the hottest thing since the mood ring. *Coincidence?* I think not.

"The whole monkey thing is *terrifying*," Kauffman contended, showing the sort of wild insensitivity that has caused us countless communication breakdowns during our time together. "I mean, we thought it was funny when we started going down the monkey road. We had no idea how many stories we'd get out of it and, even more, we had no intention of him becoming the seventh friend. I mean, we had people coming up to us saying 'Love the show. Love the monkey.' "

Why the hell not? Sister, that "monkey road"—to use your condescending, demeaning phrase—just happens to be paved with *gold*. And while I'm glad we're back on speaking terms, something still gnaws at me. I was cute enough to entertain your kids like some trained freaking animal, wasn't I? So how come I'm not good enough to be your real friend, huh? Is it just because I'm not your kind?

In the interest of balance, we all have our accounts of when things went bad—the whole thing gets to be like *Rashomon* with fur.

"There was one moment when things really turned around for the monkey," asserted Kauffman, referring to me once again in the annoying third-nonperson form. "It was the day David Schwimmer was giving him a lot of worms and the monkey sort of spit it all up. There was a live worm in the middle of the mess. The cast said, 'That's it.' That was the end of the monkey. Before that, Schwimmer was having problems with the monkey, but the rest of them were dealing with things." My own take on this regrettable incident? Simply what we party animals in the entertainment biz kindly call "creative differences."

Wherever you choose to place the blame, there's one point I'd like to get across to all the young mammals out there seeking wisdom in this book— look elsewhere, kiddos. Just kidding. No, really, what I want to say is that despite all the supposed glamour of TV, the reality ain't all big bucks, beautiful babes, and all the worms you can eat. Sure, the money's pretty good, the groupies are friendly, and all the other perks are hard to beat. But fundamentally it's hard work. And on *Friends*, all of us suffered under working conditions that could be described as . . . primitive.

Some suffered more than others. Personally, I wouldn't put an animal even lower on the evolution scale in the dressing room Todd Stevens assigned me. Of course, now that I'm back to hitting the pavement, driving my forest-green Jeep Cherokee from audition to audition, the old gang's moved on to a much plusher new studio space. Listen, I'm not bellyaching here because I'm jealous. Whatever work I'm doing these days, whether features or episodic, I know full well that it sure beats organ-grinding. All I can say is, hey, *you* try sharing a bathroom with LeBlanc, Perry, and Schwimmer sometime.

Many times when I'm approached by fans—which happens whenever I hang out in local coffeehouses with my *Friends* cast T-shirt on—they often nervously ask me, "Marcel, man to monkey, what do you really think makes the show work? How exactly does the *Friends* gang do the telegenic voodoo that you do?"

Lately, I've told these fine people that they're going to have to wait like everyone else and buy this book—hey, I ain't giving this shit away.

Now, after doing a great deal of soul-searching and hashing things out with all my old colleagues, I believe I've come up with a few insightful theories. First of all, I like to think that, for once, *Friends* offered a real situation comedy ensemble, a balanced story about seven friends, including the one who just happened to be a little hairier than all the others. When the show started, many pundits predicted *Friends* would, in short order, become Monica/Courteney's show, with the other characters restricted to the comedic sidelines.

As Lisa Kudrow confessed to *Rolling Stone*, "I thought it probably was going to be like Courteney was the Mary Tyler Moore of the show. She'd be the hub, and everything would be seen through her eyes. She'd be the normal one that everyone could identify with, and we'd all be the wacky ones. But it turned out to be a true ensemble."

"When we started," Marta confided in me, "we thought Phoebe and Chandler were not going to provide stories. But Matthew and Lisa are so great that suddenly there were lots of stories about them."

"You could see how some people saw Monica as the hub," observed David Crane. "It's her brother, her pal from high school, her apartment. But *Friends* was *always* a show about the group."

"It should be like the Beatles, and you can tell something about someone by who their favorite friend is," Marta has said. "Only with our gang, there is no lead singer."

And with *Friends*, they're all the Cute One.

"Everyone knows someone like one of the characters," Courteney explained, "and everyone's bound to like at least one of us."

"I can't think of another true ensemble that's ever worked before," David Crane claimed. "There's always a Ted Danson and Shelley Long or Judd Hirsch who really carries more of the load."

Kevin disagreed. "I think *The Beverly Hillbillies* was a true ensemble," he said, "because it really wasn't Jed's story."

Another factor in the success of *Friends* is the show's distinctive style and lightning speed. If you don't like one joke, don't worry—another one will be along shortly. According to Marta, "We knew we wanted to do something different. We wanted *Friends* to play more like a movie than a TV show, with lots and lots and lots of scenes. It's fast and cinematic, with an over-caffeinated feel. That's part of where the coffeehouse thing came in. When we first came up with the idea of a coffeehouse, that gave us a feeling of hanging out, talking, feeling overcaffeinated."

James Burrows calls the show's style "terrifically vignettety." Hey, give the guy a break, he's a big-time director, he's *supposed* to talk that way.

As for the big bosses themselves, Kauffman, Bright, and Crane have found that, in Crane's words, "it's a wonderful combination because I think we're all playing to our strengths, and there's enough overlap."

"We respect one another's opinions enormously," explained Kauffman. "We trust one another implicitly. We each have our strengths and our loves and, fortunately, they lie in different areas."

"David and I do a lot of the writing, but he stays in the writer's room," Marta revealed. "Kevin does a lot more hands-on actual production."

"Marta and I do casting," Bright noted.

"Artistic choices on the stage we do together," said Marta. "And I spend a lot of time on the stage working with the actors."

"We found that we complemented one another really well," Bright observed. "I had no desire to write, and they're the best writers I ever worked with."

But the question remains: Apart from style, what profound and previously unidentified societal need has *Friends* tapped into?

"I hope it's two things," Marta told me. "One is that it's just funny. The other is that in the stories we tell, we try to find emotional things that anyone can relate to. If they're not going through that, they probably know someone who is."

As David Crane pointed out, you can't dismiss the pure likability of the characters. "These are just people you want to be with, like the people on *Seinfeld* or *Cheers*," he told me. "I think that's true of pretty much any successful sitcom."

"Everyone can relate to one or more characters," said Matt LeBlanc. "It's a time of your life you're either looking forward to, living through, or looking back on. *Everyone* is going through this turnstile."

NBC Entertainment President Warren Littlefield has pointed out that this universality helps to explain why the show's appeal extends far beyond Generation X. "My mother feels the same way about the show as my kids do," the big guy told me.

"We found in doing the show that people care less about seeing Chandler and his boss than they do in seeing what happens when you stick Chandler and Phoebe in a room together," said Kauffman. "Any combination of the six will do. It's a hard lesson to learn, but we're so much better off when we're doing stories among our friends."

This is partly the reason the friends don't seem to work terribly hard on the show. "The problem with the workplace is that it isolates the cast," Bright elaborated, "and the strength of the show is them as a group." As one sinfully underutilized seventh wheel, I can personally vouch for this assertion myself.

And so the unstoppable *Friends* juggernaut continues. For whatever reasons, the people dig it. At watercoolers and at every exit on the Superinformation Highway, people are talking about and laughing about the show.

"When the audiences at the tapings started laughing even at the lines that weren't funny, I knew *something* was happening," Courteney told me.

Maybe that helps explain why "I'll Be There for You," that incredibly infectious theme song by the Rembrandts, is such a tremendous smash. Of course, it sure can't hurt that the track sounds so much like the Monkees.

With all this extraordinary, much-deserved success comes the threat of a backlash. However, as Marta confessed to me with a laugh, "We are not prepared for *any* backlash. I think our desperate need to be liked . . ."

"Supersedes anything else," said Crane, finishing his partner's sentence.

"Yes, the success of the first season creates a higher expectation," Kevin told me, "so we won't be able to rest on what happened the first year. Expectations are going to go up, and we'll figure out how to deliver on that."

And contrary to some previous harsh comments falsely attributed to me, I have no doubt that *Friends* will flourish without me. Does that hurt? Yeah, sure, a little bit, but I take my recovery day by day with little baby steps. To be frank, I think the most difficult thing for me will be seeing some of my old colleagues at all the fancy black-tie award ceremonies, picking up *their* Emmys and—the way things are going—Grammys, Pulitzers, and Nobel Peace Prizes too. Would it really kill the others to invite me along to accept some of the benefits of my hard-earned labors? God knows, I've already *got* the monkey suit.

To the old gang, if you happen to be reading this, there's something this humble chimp has to get off his chest: For what it's worth, after all the fights, all the tense on-set confrontations, and all those unfortunate incidents of cast members slipping on banana peels, I *still* consider each and every one of you to be my true friends.

And despite what I may have written here in the pursuit of a little product-pushing talk-show bait, I want you to know that when all is said and done, deep down, I like you. I *really* like you. Here's hoping we can sit down and break bread soon, and hey, while we're at it, do some sort of reunion special, maybe a feature?

That's what friends are for.

Location, Location, Location

Okay, so just *maybe* we buy that the friends aren't all sleeping together, but in real life they'd not be sleeping together in *much* smaller apartments, wouldn't they?

According to Manhattan realtors, roomy two-bedroom West Village pads like those seen on *Friends* can go for $1,800 to $5,000 a month. In the wonderful world of television, though, every New Yorker has rent control. How else can you explain, say, the Buchmans' arena-sized abode on *Mad About You*? Informed sources suggest that *Friends*' sometimes *sous*-chef Monica Geller and *latte*-slinger Rachel Green probably could never afford that spacious, well-lit place with an attractive view of Ugly Naked Guy.

"Very few waitresses live like that," says Sarah Larson of Frontier Brokerage, while Donna Lentol of Real Renters reports that she recently had a two-bedroom on West Tenth Street go for $3,100 a month. "And it didn't even have the character of the one on the show," she adds.

How exactly do the friends pay their rent anyway? Forget about the temp-for-life Chandler and wannabe actor Joey. An assistant chef at, say, the ultra-groovy Iridium restaurant might make $30,000 to $37,000 a year, while a coffeehouse waitress like Rachel might take home about $75 dollars at the end of the night. Go ahead, you do the math.

Well, maybe the friends' folks help out? Chandler's mom is a best-selling author, after all, and Elliott Gould *was* married to Barbra. Perhaps the whole thing's a conspiracy to promote moving to New York by people who, after all, live in Los Angeles. There is, of course, a more practical explanation: The sad truth is that the average New York apartment may be big enough for thousands of cockroaches, but not for a four-camera shoot with an ensemble cast.

A Little Friendly Competition

The Totally Twirly Quiz

MULTIPLE CHOICE

**1) Which of the following is *not* a title that was considered for
     Friends?**

a) *Insomnia Café*

b) *Six of One*

c) *Across the Hall*

d) *Once Upon a Time in the West Village*

**2) Which was the first line of dialogue in the *Friends* pilot
     episode?**

a) "Anyone wanna pet my monkey?"

b) "Hey, kids, let's change the face of television forever."

c) "There's nothing to tell."

d) "Thank you for being a friend."

**3) Where were Rachel and Barry planning to go on their
     honeymoon?**

a) The Orthodontia Hall of Fame in Cooperstown

b) Aruba

c) A Princess cruise

d) The Ugly Naked Guy Nudist Colony

**4) Which of the following does Marcel hump in
     "The One with the Fake Monica"?**

a) Ross' leg

b) Rachel's Curious George doll

c) A lamp

d) All of the above

**5) What's the title of the musical Joey appears in during
     "The One with the Butt"?**

a) *Freud!*

b) *Waterworld: The Musical*

c) *Franz Kafka's The Metamorphosis*

d) *Katz*

6) At Chandler's office, what does WENUS stand for?

a) Wasted Energy Negotiation Union Service

b) Wacky Environment National User Station

c) Weekly Estimate Net Usage System

d) Western Electric Northern Under Sales

7) Which *Friends* character hits on Rachel in the first episode?
a) Joey
b) Mr. Heckles
c) Marcel
d) Phoebe

8) According to Ross in "The One with the Blackout," where's the weirdest place he's ever had sex?
a) New Jersey
b) The White House
c) Disneyland
d) The Vatican

9) Chandler's coworker Shelly mistakenly assumes he's . . .
a) Jewish
b) Gay
c) Fired
d) A terrorist

10) Which of the following friends were invited to Rachel's wedding to Barry?
a) Just Monica
b) Monica and Ross
c) Joey and Marcel
d) None of the above

11) Which New York museum does Ross work at?
a) The Manhattan Museum of the Mensch
b) The Museum of Natural History
c) The Museum of Broadcasting
d) The West Village Monkey Museum

12) Who of the following has never appeared in an episode of *Friends*?
a) Jon Lovitz
b) Jay Leno
c) Dick Clark
d) Johnnie Cochran

13) Who can be seen on a poster in Chandler and Joey's apartment?
a) David Copperfield
b) Nine Inch Nails
c) Joseph Stalin
d) Laurel and Hardy

14) In "The One Where Nana Dies Twice," where does Jack Geller tell his daughter Monica that he wants to be buried?
a) In Grant's Tomb
b) At sea
c) Under Central Perk
d) On a competing network

15) What's Marcel's favorite song?
a) "Mickey's Monkey"
b) "Jungle Boogie"
c) "The Lion Sleeps Tonight"
d) "I'll Be There for You"

16) What does Ross and Monica's grandmother Nana collect?
a) NutraSweets
b) Autographs
c) Stamps
d) Sweet'n Lows

17) With the help of Monica's brief love interest Alan, the gang beats which of these teams at softball?

a) The New York Mets
b) The cast of *Mad About You*
c) The Hassidic jewelers
d) The League of Women Voters

18) What does the real Monica tell the fake Monica her name is?
a) Nana
b) Monana
c) Janice
d) Bruce

19) Which of the following is a stage name that Joey uses?
a) Hal Pacino
b) Holden McGroin
c) Ishmael
d) Marcel

20) When did Chandler's parents tell him that they were divorcing?
a) During Thanksgiving dinner
b) At birth
c) While watching one of Joey's plays
d) Never

MATCHING

21) Ross and Rachel's detergent	a) *Mistress Bitch*
22) Monica's trendy restaurant	b) Minsk
23) Nora Bing's big best-seller	c) Überweiss
24) What gum would be to Chandler	d) Bobo the Sperm Guy
25) Joey's name on VD Poster	e) Mario
26) What Susan calls Ross	f) Perfection
27) Where Phoebe's science guy goes	g) Iridium
28) Joey Sr.'s mistress	h) Ethan
29) Chandler's sexy subordinate	i) Luisa
30) Animal Control's hard-liner	j) Nina Bookbinder
31) Monica's jailbait	k) Ronnie

MORE MULTIPLE CHOICE

32) For what role is Matthew Perry's actor father John Bennett Perry best known?
a) Potsie in *Happy Days*
b) The Old Spice sailor
c) The Roto-Rooter Man
d) Schneider on *One Day at a Time*

33) Men in which profession tend to attract Rachel's romantic interest?
a) Circus geeks
b) Hostage negotiators
c) Lawyers
d) Doctors

34) Which of the following is *not* a Scrabble letter that Marcel eats in "The One with Two Parts, Part Two"?

a) M
b) O
c) K
d) X

35) What's the name of Ross' childhood dog?

a) Mr. Heckles
b) Ugly Naked Dog
c) Chi Chi
d) Paolo

36) Which of the following songs has not been played on *Friends*?

a) "New York Minute" by Don Henley
b) "Shiny Happy People" by R.E.M.
c) "Everybody's Got Something to Hide Except Me and My Monkey" by The Beatles
d) "Take a Bow" by Madonna

37) Which of the following is not a TV show in which Matt LeBlanc has appeared?

a) *Red Shoe Diaries*
b) *Vinnie & Bobby*
c) *Eerie, Indiana*
d) *Top of the Heap*

38) What's the Gellers' affectionate nickname for their daughter Monica?

a) "The Thing That Ate the Tri-State Area"
b) "Our Little Harmonica"
c) "The One Who's Not Ross"
d) "Lauren"

39) Which of the following is *not* a onetime romantic interest of Rachel?

a) Barry

b) Paolo

c) Pete the Weeper

d) Jimmy the Weasel

40) Which of following is *not* a onetime love interest of Monica?

a) Paul the Wine Guy

b) Fun Bobby

c) Alan

d) Moribund Murray

41) By which date does Rachel say Paolo had named her breasts?

a) Their first date

b) Their third date

c) Their sixth date

d) Their eighth date

42) Ross' apartment has a poster showing which cartoon character?

a) Pocahontas

b) Speed Racer

c) Jughead

d) Dr. Katz: Professional Therapist

43) Which of the following was *not* a name considered for Carol and Ross' baby?

a) Jamie

b) Jordie

c) Dylan

d) Paolo

44) Which *Friends* star appeared in *Ace Ventura: Pet Detective*?

a) Marcel

b) Courteney Cox

c) David Schwimmer

d) Ugly Naked Guy

45) What's the name of the high school that Monica, Ross, and Rachel attended?
a) Ridgemont High
b) West Beverly High
c) Lincoln High
d) Sweet Valley High

46) Which rock group sings the *Friends'* theme song?
a) The Monkees
b) The Foo Fighters
c) The Rembrandts
d) Toad the Wet Sprocket

47) What actress plays Gloria Tribbiani, Joey's mother?
a) Elinor Donahue
b) Telma Hopkins
c) Vanessa Redgrave
d) Brenda Vaccaro

48) Which of the following is *not* a TV show on which Matthew Perry has appeared?
a) *Boys Will Be Boys*
b) *Charles in Charge*
c) *Beverly Hills 90210*
d) *Family Matters*

49) What comedy troupe once claimed Lisa Kudrow as a member?
a) The Kids in the Hall
b) The Committee
c) The Groundlings
d) The State

50) Where does Marcel end up going?
a) The Bronx Zoo
b) The San Diego Zoo
c) The Great Neck Zoo
d) The Screen Actors' Retirement Home

TRUE OR FALSE:

51) Monica and Phoebe were college roommates.

52) Marcel once got Monica and Phoebe's TV stuck in Yiddish mode.

53) Monica had a crush on Joey when he first moved in.

54) Joey occasionally cooks nude.

55) Chandler and Ross went to college together.

56) Telly Savalas was Jennifer Aniston's godfather.

57) Lisa Kudrow starred in the brief TV version of *Cabin Boy*.

58) Ross works as an anthropologist.

59) Ross' ex-wife Carol is a schoolteacher.

REAL OR FAKE FRIENDS: Which of the following are actual *Friends* episodes and which are made up?

60) "The One with the Boobies"

61) "The One with Salman Rushdie"

62) "The One Where Underdog Gets Away"

63) "The One Where Absolutely Nothing Happens"

64) "The One Where Robert Dole's Offended"

65) "The One with the Evil Orthodontist"

66) "The One Where Joey Gets His Doctorate"

67) "The One with the Rent Increase"

68) "The One with the Butt"

69) "The One with the Stoned Guy"

STILL MORE MULTIPLE CHOICE

70) Who does Rachel say resembles her ex-fiancé Barry?

a) Keanu Reeves

b) Eddie Vedder

c) Ethan Hawke

d) Mr. Potato Head

71) Which of the following actresses plays Rachel's onetime maid of honor Mindy?

a) Tina Yothers

b) Trini Alvarado

c) Jennifer Grey

d) Susan Olsen

72) What is Lizzy the homeless lady's affectionate nickname for Phoebe, who gives her $1000 in "The One with the Thumb"?

a) Weird Girl
b) Space Case
c) Dysfunctional One
d) Ursula

73) Which NBC sitcom also features Jessica Hecht, who plays Carol's lover Susan on *Friends*?

a) *Caroline in the City*
b) *The Single Guy*
c) *Mad About You*
d) *Wings*

74) Which *Friends* star appears in the film *Outbreak*?

a) Matthew Perry
b) Lisa Kudrow
c) Elliott Gould
d) Marcel

75) Which of the following is *not* a show on which Jennifer Aniston has appeared?

a) *Muddling Through*
b) *All American Girl*
c) *The Edge*
d) *Ferris Bueller*

NAME THAT FRIEND

76) The one who has a twin sister

77) The one who was fat growing up

78) The one who's been kissed by Jill Goodacre

79) The one who once worked at Macy's

80) The one who goes to China for a "bone thing"

81) The one who cuts up his/her credit cards

82) The one whose engagement ring gets lost in lasagna

83) The one who falls in a grave

84) The one whose mother kisses Ross romantically

85) The one whose dad's having an affair

86) The one who sings at Central Perk

87) The one who works at Central Perk

88) The one who had a lisping boyfriend named Steve

89) The one who gets struck by a hockey puck

MORE TRUE OR FALSE

90) George Stephanopoulos can be seen in the episode "The One with George Stephanopoulos."

91) Joey has a sister named Tina.

92) The exterior of the apartment building seen on *Friends* can actually be found in Los Angeles.

93) Chandler has broken up with Janice on both Valentine's Day and New Year's Eve.

94) Rachel Green has a sister.

EVEN MORE MULTIPLE CHOICE

95) **Which of the following is *not* a TV show that the friends have watched onscreen?**

a) *Laverne y Shirley*

b) *Happy Days*

c) A Spanish soap opera

d) *Alf*

96) **Which NBC personality did *not* appear in "The One with Two Parts"?**

a) Helen Hunt

b) George Clooney

c) Kelsey Grammer

d) Noah Wyle

97) **Which of the following is *not* among the credits of *Friends'* Executive Producers and Creators Marta Kauffman and David Crane?**

a) *Dream On*

b) *Family Album*

c) *Dr. Quinn, Medicine Woman*

d) *The Powers That Be*

98) Which of the following is *not* among the credits of *Friends'* Executive Producer Kevin S. Bright?

a) *Dream On*

b) *The Ron Reagan Show*

c) *The History of White People in America*

d) *SeaQuest DSV*

99) According to Carol, why can't the baby be called Jamie?

a) That name's already being used on *Mad About You*.

b) Susan had an old girlfriend by that name.

c) She hates the letter "J."

d) She prefers a more gender-biased name.

100) Who of the following has been seen in Central Perk?

a) Chandler's father

b) Janice

c) Roger the Shrink

d) Ugly Naked Guy

Essay Questions to Ponder (Not for Credit):

How far away do Ross and Phoebe actually live?

Exactly how do Monica and Rachel and Chandler and Joey afford those great roomy Manhattan apartments?

When did they all get to be such good friends?

ANSWERS

1) d	14) b	27) b
2) c	15) c	28) k
3) b	16) d	29) j
4) d	17) c	30) i
5) a	18) b	31) h
6) c	19) b	32) b
7) a	20) a	33) d
8) c	21) c	34) d
9) b	22) g	35) c
10) d	23) a	36) c
11) b	24) f	37) c
12) d	25) e	38) b
13) d	26) d	39) d

40) d
41) c
42) b
43) d
44) b
45) c
46) c
47) d
48) d
49) c
50) b
51) True
52) False, it was Spanish
53) True
54) True, oatmeal and toast— "nothing that splatters"
55) True
56) True
57) False
58) False
59) True

60) Real
61) Fake
62) Real
63) Fake
64) Fake
65) Real
66) Fake
67) Fake
68) Real
69) Real
70) d
71) c
72) a
73) b
74) d
75) b
76) Phoebe
77) Monica
78) Chandler
79) Joey
80) Ross
81) Rachel
82) Rachel

83) Ross
84) Chandler
85) Joey
86) Phoebe
87) Rachel
88) Monica
89) Ross
90) False
91) True
92) False, it's in New York City
93) True
94) True, Rachel says her sister's going to loan her and Paolo her house in the Poconos
95) d
96) c
97) c
98) d
99) b
100) d

SCORING
(the thing of which there's never enough on *Friends*)

Each question counts for one point.
80–100 points: Congratulations, you're an honorary friend. See you at Central Perk.
50–80 points: Take it easy—your WENUS may be lagging a bit, but you're still considered a friend of *Friends*.
20–50 points: Hey, don't worry, you've scored the same as Joey.
0–20 points: Come on, pal. Marcel got 21 right, so you have no excuse. Keep reading.

Friendsography

An Episode-by-Episode Guide to the First Season

THE PILOT

Director: James Burrows
Writers: Marta Kauffman & David Crane
Original Airdate: September 22, 1994

The mother of all *Friends* episodes opens at Central Perk, our gang-to-be's neighborhood coffeehouse hangout. Monica Geller (Courteney Cox) is discussing her upcoming date with Paul the Wine Guy with her pals Phoebe Buffay (Lisa Kudrow), Chandler Bing (Matthew Perry), and Joey Tribbiani (Matt LeBlanc). Welcome to *Friends'* very first bad date. Suddenly Monica's older brother Ross Geller (David Schwimmer) arrives looking distraught. It seems his wife Carol has just moved her stuff out—she's left him, having realized that she's made a major lifestyle mistake. "And you didn't know she was a lesbian?" Joey asks. Ross seems frustrated with this line of inquiry. "*She* didn't know," he says, "how should I know?"

Next an unexpected and thoroughly drenched Rachel Green appears wearing a wet wedding dress. Monica introduces Rachel to Phoebe, Chandler, and Joey as her fellow survivor of Lincoln High. Rachel explains that she's just run out of her wedding, dumping her fiancé Barry at the altar. "I realized I was more turned on by this gravy boat than by Barry," Rachel says by way of an explanation. "And I got really freaked out by how much Barry looked like Mr. Potato Head. You know, I mean, I always knew he looked familiar."

Soon, despite not having invited Monica to her nonwedding, Rachel manages to invite herself to stay with Monica. Now the gang's all here.

Sensitive singer-songwriter Phoebe sings a song about "raindrops on roses" to comfort Rachel, while Joey almost immediately hits on her. Monica admonishes him for coming on to a woman on her wedding day. "What?" Joey replies. "Like there's a rule or something."

Back at Monica's place—now becoming Monica and Rachel's apartment—the pop culture–loving gang watches a Spanish language soap opera and a *Happy Days* rerun. The latter TV show moves the fragile Rachel. "See but Joanie *loved* Chachi," she says. "That's the difference."

During his date with Monica, Paul the Sensitive Wine Guy confesses that he can't perform sexually ever since his wife left him. This will turn out to be a highly effective Big Lie, and a unique seduction strategy.

Back at the apartment the somewhat spoiled Rachel asks the gang, "So, like, you guys all have jobs?" Monica gives her a tough-love lesson in Economics 101. "Yeah, we all have jobs. See, that's how we . . . buy stuff." Rachel finds out—as do we all—that Joey's a struggling actor whose most impressive credits include a Wee Ones production of *Pinocchio*.

At work as a chef at an elegant uptown restaurant, Monica finds out her coworker Franny also has swallowed Paul's impotency line as well.

Rachel also gets to hear some of Phoebe's twisted history. "Pheebs" came to the city at fourteen; her mom had killed herself, and her stepfather was back in prison. She ended up living with an albino guy who cleaned windshields outside the Port Authority. Then he killed himself and she discovered aromatherapy. Faced with this epic tale of dysfunction, Rachel has no reply.

The gang begins to bring out new strengths in Rachel. "Come on," Monica tells her, "you can't live off your parents your whole life." Rachel responds, "I know that! That's why I was getting married!" By episode's end, she'll start working at Central Perk. And in a declaration of independence, Rachel cuts up her credit cards. "Welcome to the real world," Monica tells her. "It sucks. You're gonna love it."

In a significant moment, Ross admits to Rachel that he had a crush on her back in high school. She's not surprised. He asks her if he could ask her out sometime. Rachel answers, "Yeah, maybe."

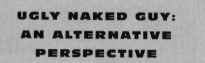

THE ONE WITH THE SONOGRAM AT THE END

Director: James Burrows
Writers: Marta Kauffman & David Crane
Original Airdate: September 29, 1994

In "The One with the Sonogram at the End" *Friends* establishes that it will be a sort of family show for the nineties.

At Central Perk, the guys and girls discuss the differing attitudes of men and women regarding the role of kissing in sexual relations. Rachel says that kissing is as important as any other part. Chandler explains that for men kissing's more like an opening act, like "the comedian you have to sit through before Pink Floyd comes out."

Paleontologist Ross, who works at the Museum of Natural History, is there talking with his colleague Marsha (comedy writer Merrill Markoe) when he sees his wife Carol Willick. (Carol is played in this episode by Anita Barone while in subsequent shows she'll be replaced by Jane Sibbert.) Carol's come by to tell Ross that she's pregnant. Carol assures Ross that she and her lover Susan Bunch (Jessica Hecht) want him "to be involved"—if he wants to be.

Ugly Naked Guy—the friends' unseen neighbor whom they often spot in the window of a nearby apartment building—makes his first non-appearance in this episode. Today his acquisition and apparent usage of a Thighmaster disgusts the gang. As Monica's compulsiveness is addressed—with Phoebe referring to her as getting all "twirly"—things take a dark turn when Rachel briefly loses the engagement ring she's going to give back to Barry in lasagna.

We discover that Monica's freaked

UGLY NAKED GUY: AN ALTERNATIVE PERSPECTIVE

Consider for just a moment how *Friends* must look from the point of view of *Friends*' best-loved unseen character (one who has one-upped Rhoda's invisible Carlton the Doorman by not having a speaking part either). What must it be like for this friendly nudist neighbor to live so close yet so far from the *Friends* action? It's sort of *Rear Window* for Generation X. Here (just across the street) is a smash spin-off series waiting to happen.

TERMS OF ENDEARMENT

Twirly (adjective)—Phoebe's word to describe Monica's hyperobsessive behavior, as in "all chaotic and twirly."

out by her parents—the affable if slightly insensitive Jack Geller (Elliott Gould) and the pushy, hypercritical Judy Geller (Christina Pickles). It turns out that Monica's older brother Ross is the long-reigning prince of the Geller family. "Apparently, there was some ceremony before I was born," explains Monica. It turns out that Monica was a chubby and not particularly popular kid. Still, Dad warmly calls her "our little Harmonica."

For the first time, Phoebe mentions that she has a "high-powered" twin sister—Ursula the waitress, who the rest of us already know from *Mad About You.*

Ross goes with Carol and Susan to her OB/GYN, Dr. Oberman, and they argue over the baby's name. Susan has proposed "Helen." Ross doesn't think Helen Geller works. It turns out that Susan wants *her* last name, Bunch, in the mix too. More tense arguments ensue, until they all see a sonogram of the baby and all three of them are moved by the sight of their child to be.

Rachel goes to the jilted Barry's office, only to find him tanned and happy, having gone on their honeymoon with her maid of honor Mindy.

Back at Monica and Rachel's everyone watches a videotape of the sonogram. "What are we supposed to be seeing here," Joey asks. "I don't know," says Chandler, "but I think it's about to attack the *Enterprise.*"

Note: The opening sequence to this episode originally featured the cast dancing and frolicking around the fountain without footage from assorted episodes. This frolicking was shot on the Warner Bros. lot.

THE ONE WITH THE THUMB

Director: James Burrows
Writers: Jeffrey Astrof & Mike Sikowitz
Original Airdate: October 6, 1994

The show opens with the much put-upon Ross being dealt yet another blow: In a conversation at Central Perk he discovers all these years later that despite what his parents told him, his beloved childhood dog Chi Chi didn't *really* go off to the Milners' farm in Connecticut. (Chi Chi's dead, that's what I said.)

COFFEE TALK: Rachel, Monica, and Chandler in their natural environment in "The One with the Thumb"

Chandler—who had quit cigarettes sometime in the past—gets hooked again on smoking while helping Joey rehearse some lines for a play. Meanwhile, much to her apparent frustration, Phoebe keeps mistakenly getting money that's not rightfully hers from her bank, first $500 extra, then, even more annoyingly to her, $1000.

Monica discusses her reluctance to have all her friends meet her new guy, Alan. She implies that the group was unfairly tough on another fellow, Steve, who apparently had a lisping problem. She needn't worry. As it turns out, the gang all completely *love* Alan (Geoffrey Lower). Even the hard-to-please Chandler praises Alan's impression of David Hasselhoff, while Ross likes most "the way he makes me feel about myself." Remarkably it appears that Alan has swept everyone off their feet . . . with the unfortunate exception of Monica. Still the gang continues to collectively fall for Alan, especially after the guy excels in their historic softball victory over the Hassidic jewelers.

Phoebe decides to give the extra money she's gotten to Lizzy, a homeless woman who appropriately dubs Phoebe "Weird Girl."

Lizzy insists on buying Weird Girl a soda in return for her generous gift, and Phoebe proceeds to find a detached thumb in the can. For her trouble, Phoebe receives $7000 from the soda company. Finally, she offers to give this money to Chandler if only he'll stop smoking. No fool he, Bing jumps at the healthy payday.

Later, Phoebe and Rachel are watching Shari Lewis and Lamb Chop on television when Monica rounds up all the friends and breaks the news—she's going to split up with Alan. Sadly, the gang takes the news hard. Ironically, Alan reacts a little better. He'll miss Monica, but as he confesses to her, "I just can't stand your friends."

THE ONE WITH GEORGE STEPHANOPOULOS

Director: James Burrows
Writer: Alexa Junge
Original Airdate: October 13, 1994

Here *Friends* suggests that politics can indeed make dreamy bedfellows. While hanging out at Central Perk, the gang discusses what they'd all do "if I were omnipotent for a day." Confusing the word with impotence, Joey explains that he would probably kill himself.

Phoebe's grandmother has a new boyfriend and they're so loud in bed that it's hard for Phoebe to sleep at her place. So Monica and Rachel invite her for a sleep-over. Joey and Chandler meanwhile offer Ross a ticket to a hockey game. Ross becomes particularly depressed when he realizes that it's the anniversary of when Carol and he first consummated their physical relationship. Eventually, he admits to the guys that Carol was his first— and only—lover.

THE GAMES PEOPLE PLAY: A game of friendly Twister breaks out in "The One with George Stephanopoulos"

Rachel gets her first paycheck for waitressing at Central Perk, and after some initial excitement, certain painful fiscal realities hit her hard. Seeing all the money taken out for taxes, she reasonably asks, "Who's FICA? Why is he getting my money?"

Just then a pack of Rachel's rich women friends turn up at Central Perk—pregnant Leslie, bubbly Kiki, and acerbic Joanne. To say the least, Monica and Phoebe are not impressed with this gaggle of alternative friends. By the same token, these well-heeled ladies don't seem too impressed with Rachel's new, more grungy life.

As Monica, Rachel, and Phoebe get ready for their slumber party, a Visa representative calls because they noticed some unusual activity on Rachel's account—*none*. During the party—which finds the women drinking Tiki

Death Punch—the pizza delivery guy tells them he doesn't have their fat-free with extra cheese pizza. Their order has been switched with that of George Stephanopoulos, who apparently lives across the street. With much sexual excitement, the women (all apparently Friends of Bill) rush to spot George with binoculars.

True confessions break out among the tipsy lady friends— Monica once made Phoebe a vegetarian pâté that wasn't vegetarian, Phoebe slept with a guy named Jason Hurley only hours after he and Monica broke up. Once again they address the fact that Monica was once fat. "She was a big girl," says Rachel, who admits to having once put a fake valentine in her locker from one Tommy Rollerson.

LADIES' NIGHT IN: The women enjoy a little Tiki Death Punch in "The One with George Stephanopoulos"

At the New York Rangers hockey game, poor Ross gets hit in the nose by a flying puck, smashing and shattering his nose. In the emergency room the guys encounter sadist Nurse Sizemore. Happily by episode's end, the nurse gets accidentally beaned by Ross' hockey puck.

PUCKING UP: Ross gets involved in the hockey game in "The One with George Stephanopoulos"

THE ONE WITH THE EAST GERMAN LAUNDRY DETERGENT

Director: Pam Fryman
Writers: Jeff Greenstein & Jeff Strauss
Original Airdate: October 20, 1994

This *Friends* is truly a romantic and cleansing affair with a Germanic twist.

After an opening conversation about male-female relations, Chandler explains that he has to try to break up with oh-so-annoying girlfriend Janice (Maggie Wheeler). Phoebe says that she'll join him and break up with a beau named Tony. Meanwhile, on the phone Rachel's dad offers her a Mercedes convertible to come home.

Back at the coffeehouse Joey sees Angela, a woman he had recently broken up with, and suddenly decides he wants her back again. Unfortunately, she's now with some guy named Bob. Joey lies and claims that Monica is his girlfriend, then tricks her into going on a fake double date. A reluctant Monica is led to believe that Bob is Angela's brother as well as her date for the evening.

Back home, Ugly Naked Guy is spotted laying kitchen tiles.

Ross and Rachel have an intimate laundry date planned, and in Ross' bedroom—seen for the first time here—Chandler cautions Ross not to bring dirty underwear and Snuggle fabric softener to the laundromat.

Later at Central Perk, Janice—she of the annoying laugh—surprises Chandler with a cute little gift, Bullwinkle socks. She knows that he already has the Rocky ones. Before Chandler can even get his breakup under way, Phoebe and Tony complete a shockingly graceful split with a friendly hug. To put it mildly, Janice doesn't take the news well. Chandler cannot comfort her. Eventually, Phoebe saves the day by working her breakup magic on Janice, who finally leaves Central Perk calmly.

FRIENDLY BANTER

On *The Tonight Show*, Jay Leno asked Jennifer Aniston to touch her tongue to her nose. "This is a rare, *rare* talent," he said. "On cable there are some women that can do it. But there are none I understand in network TV that have that talent." Aniston politely declined but promised to perform the act the next time she appeared.

At the laundromat, Rachel and Ross battle a Horrible Woman—the script even identifies her as such. Ross offers Rachel his detergent Überweiss, explaining, "It's new. It's German. It's extra tough." Rachel confesses to being a "laundry virgin." Ross' intense feelings for Rachel are very clear now, except to Rachel. She meanwhile sees doing laundry as a significant sign of her independence. So she's crushed when she discovers she left a red sock in with her whites and as a result everything's pink. "I'm going to look like a big marshmallow peep," she exclaims in horror. "What am I doing? My father's right. I can't live on my own. I can't even do laundry." Happily, Rachel gets her confidence back by facing down Horrible Woman over a laundry cart. Excited, she kisses Ross' cheek in victory. To Ross this is clearly a big deal—their first kiss.

Over dinner, Monica sees Bob and Angela making out and is thoroughly disgusted until she realizes that Joey has scammed her. Thinking quickly, Joey convinces Monica—who's attracted to Bob—that together they can break the couple up. She flirts with Bob. Joey plies Angela with chicken wings. And it works.

FRIENDLY LOOKS

In the article "Style Secrets of Those Trendy *Friends*" from the November 1995 issue of *Celebrity Hair*, *Friends*' stylist Janet Medford described Jennifer Aniston's massively popular shag hairstyle as "a little bit below the shoulder and layered all over. The layers are not long . . . not like in the eighties when everybody had the short, layered look on top. It's longer on the top, then shags toward the bottom." When *Celebrity Hair* asked her, "Is that the trend in hair now?" Medford said, "Absolutely! Yes, that's the new look and actually, the girls on *Friends* are pretty much the trendsetters right now, I think. Whatever they're doing is what's happening now." Just how happening the *Friends* hair had truly become was clear when *People* profiled Chris McMillan of L.A.'s Estilo salon as the man responsible for the *Friends* women's influential cuts in September. "He's got a vision," Lisa Kudrow told the magazine. "He creates hair sculptures."

THE ONE WITH THE BUTT

Director: Arlene Sanford
Writers: Adam Chase & Ira Ungerleider
Original Airdate: October 27, 1994

Friends goes to the theater!

Those supportive friends attend Joey's latest play, a horrific-looking musical called *Freud!* There Chandler spots a beautiful woman named Aurora (Sofia Milos). He asks her out and is pleasantly surprised when she says yes. Aurora turns out to be exotic and highly interesting. She was in the Israeli army. She's perfect for Chandler . . . except for the fact that she's married to someone named Rick. And she has a boyfriend named Ethan.

Monica reacts badly to Rachel cleaning the apartment and moving some things around, including her green ottoman. The gang confronts the fastidious Monica with how anal she is. "When we were kids, yours was the only Raggedy Ann doll that wasn't raggedy," her big brother points out.

A thrilled Joey announces he's going to work with his hero Al Pacino—as Al's personal butt double. "After all your struggling, you've finally been able to crack your way into show business," says a butt-kissing Chandler. Joey entertains everyone by performing Al lines from . . . *And Justice for All* and *The Godfather, Part III*. Sadly, on the movie set, Joey and the director seem to disagree on the butt's motivation in the shower scene. Joey's very Method-influenced, it seems. Interestingly, the director in this scene—who calls Joey "Butt Guy"—is played by famed TV director James Burrows even though he wasn't behind the camera for this particular *Friends* episode.

Aurora breaks the news to Chandler that she's seeing another man—her fourth guy in current rotation. Reluctantly, Chandler decides he can't deal with the situation.

Later, the gang comforts a downbeat Joey. Phoebe turns his mood around by telling him that he's got to keep on believing that someday a kid's going to say, "I'm going to be Joey Tribbiani's ass."

WHISTLE A FRIENDLY TUNE

"I'll Be There for You" (theme from *Friends*) is the sort of unbelievably infectious pop song sure to cheer you up when it hasn't been your day, your week, your month, or even your year. Yes, it's wonderfully retro-sounding, and intentionally so. "I grew up on The Monkees and The Beatles and was very influenced by that stuff for 'I'll Be There for You,'" says Michael Skloff, one of the composers of the hugely popular song. According to Skloff, early models for the song were The Beatles' classics "Paperback Writer" and "I Feel Fine."

"For the show's opening sequence, we originally only did a forty-five-second version," recalls Skloff, a composer married to *Friends* co-creator Marta Kauffman. *Friends* executive producer Kevin S. Bright, a major music buff, brought in lyricist Allee Willis to contribute to the theme song and came up with the idea of getting the Rembrandts—the talented pop-rock duo of Danny Wilde and Phil Solem—to sing it. Before long, the popularity of "I'll Be There for You" was exploding, with disc jockeys starting to tape the tune off the television and play it—hand claps and all—on the air. Clearly the demand was there for a full-length version, and so the song was extended with additional lyrics by Kauffman, David Crane, Wilde, and Solem. The rest is pop history. "I'll Be There for You" can now be heard on the *Friends* sound-track album, which also includes contributions from R.E.M., Lou Reed, k. d. lang, Paul Westerberg, Joni Mitchell, Hootie and the Blowfish, Toad the Wet Sprocket, Barenaked Ladies, and Grant Lee Buffalo.

THE ONE WITH THE BLACKOUT

Director: James Burrows
Writers: Jeffrey Astrof & Mike Sikowitz
Original Airdate: November 3, 1994

In the opening of this widely acknowledged *Friends* classic, a blackout hits when all the friends except Chandler are at Central Perk. As it turns out, the fortunate Mr. Bing finds himself trapped in an ATM vestibule with that famed Victoria's Secret model Jill Goodacre. Chandler will spend much of the episode trying to figure out a way to capitalize on this stroke of blackout luck.

Back at the apartment building, Joey lights a menorah—he explains that Chandler's old roommate was Jewish. Across the way, Ugly Naked Guy lights candles and burns himself.

The gang discusses the weirdest place they've ever had sex. Monica says that for her it was senior year of college on a pool table. Joey reports that he once had relations in the women's room on the second floor of the New York Public Library. "Oh my God," says a shocked Monica, "what were *you* doing in a library?" Phoebe explains that the weirdest place she ever had sex was Milwaukee. For Ross it was the time he and Carol did it at Disneyland in 1989.

BIG TALKER: Ross plans his big move on Rachel in "The One with the Blackout"

Apparently, and appropriately, they were subsequently barred from the Magic Kingdom. The relatively unadventurous Rachel says she once had sex at the foot of the bed. She bemoans the lack of passion in her life. Ross meaningfully tells her, "I see a big passion in your future." Rachel doesn't get the hint.

Seeing what's going on in Ross' mind regarding Rachel, Joey tells him, "It's never gonna happen. Now you're in the Friend Zone." Ross tries to protest. "Ross, you're *mayor* of the Zone," Joey insists.

Back at the ATM vestibule, Chandler passes on an offer of gum from Jill. Much to his chagrin, things initially go rather awkwardly between them. After a time, an unusually tongue-tied Chandler tells Jill he's changed his mind: "You know, on second thought, gum would be perfection."

As the other friends hang out in the dark back home, Phoebe lets on that Monica had a crush on Joey when he was first moving in. Later while Phoebe leads Joey and Monica in a rendition of "Top of the World," outside on the balcony Ross is about to tell Rachel of his feelings when a cat jumps on him and the fur flies.

Rachel and Phoebe look for the cat's owner. Their weird neighbor Mr. Heckles (Larry Hankin) claims

the cat is his and that its name is Bob Buttons. Clearly, he's lying and the cat runs away. While searching for the cat, Rachel is thrilled to run into its studly Italian owner Paolo (Cosimo Fusco). Soon she brings Paolo back to her apartment to meet the friends. Ross is *not* pleased.

Trying pitifully to impress Jill by blowing a bubble, a nervous Chandler eventually ends up choking.

Back in the apartment, all the women are turned on by Paolo despite the fact that

he barely speaks English. Ross attempts to get Paolo to back off, saying that he and Rachel are "together" even though "the sex is not being had." Later, the girls' candles run out and when lights come back on Rachel and Paolo are kissing.

In their post-choke era, Jill and Chandler finally bond. When she leaves with a kiss, Chandler turns to the ATM camera, gives his account number, and requests a video.

Note: Jill Goodacre is married in real life to musician Harry Connick, Jr. According to the credits, "The One with the Blackout" guest stars Jill Connick as Jill Goodacre.

THE ONE WHERE NANA DIES TWICE

Director: James Burrows
Writers: Marta Kauffman & David Crane
Original Airdate: November 10, 1995

In "The One Where Nana Dies Twice," the viewer grapples with matters of human sexuality and death, and still exits laughing.

Chandler's coworker Shelly approaches him about the possibility of setting him up with someone—a man, as it turns out. She had assumed that

A BIG WENUS: Chandler enjoys a rare gratifying office moment

Chandler was gay. When he goes back to Monica and Rachel's apartment and tells them, the women surprise him by admitting that they'd had the same misconception of him early on. The guys didn't share that suspicion, though Ross admits to having told Susan Salidor—a girl he liked in college—that Chandler was seeing Bernie Spellman, another fellow who liked her. Chandler is blown away and wants to know why they thought he was gay. The consensus is that he "has a quality."

As Rachel talks to Paolo from Rome on the phone, Jack Geller beeps in with news that Judy's mother Nana is dying. Even at the hospital, mother Judy drives Monica crazy. "What's with your hair?" her mother asks. Ross attempts to calm his little sister down. "Relax. Okay, we're gonna be here for a while, it looks like, and we still have 'boyfriends' and 'your career' to cover," he tells her. Monica and Ross' Aunt Lillian (played by Elinor Donahue of *Father Knows Best* fame) is there as well.

They all talk about Nana, and fondly recall her hoarding of Sweet'n Lows. After being told she's dead by a nurse, Ross and Monica go to her bedside for a final good-bye. Suddenly Nana revives, albeit briefly. "This almost never happens," the nurse tells them. Later while looking for clothes for Nana to be buried in, Ross comes across Nana's vast artificial sweetener collection in her closet, as well as his old retainer.

Chandler finds out that the fellow Shelly wanted to set him up with was Lowell in Financial Services. Getting momentarily caught up in the issue, Chandler opines that Brian in Payroll would be a *much* better choice. Shelly says Brian's out of his league.

At the cemetery during Nana's funeral, ever-sensitive Joey watches the Giants/Cowboys football game. Ross falls in an open grave and hurts himself. High as a kite on painkillers at the post-funeral reception, Ross tries again to tell Rachel he loves her, and fails to make his point yet again.

In a nearly heart-to-heart mother-daughter chat, Judy tells Monica how critical her own mother, Nana, was of everything that she did. Clearly the good old

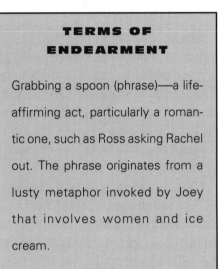

TERMS OF ENDEARMENT

Grabbing a spoon (phrase)—a life-affirming act, particularly a romantic one, such as Ross asking Rachel out. The phrase originates from a lusty metaphor invoked by Joey that involves women and ice cream.

cycle of family pain continues. The gang looks at a picture of Nana with her friends back in 1939 when she was their age. "It looks like a fun gang," Ross tells his own pals.

At Chandler's office the next day, Lowell says he knew Chandler wasn't gay, but tells him that *yes*, Brian is—and way out of his league. Chandler's in the process of debating the point when Brian happens by.

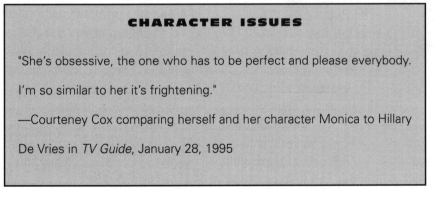

CHARACTER ISSUES

"She's obsessive, the one who has to be perfect and please everybody. I'm so similar to her it's frightening."

—Courteney Cox comparing herself and her character Monica to Hillary De Vries in *TV Guide*, January 28, 1995

THE ONE WHERE UNDERDOG GETS AWAY

Director: James Burrows
Writers: Jeff Greenstein & Jeff Strauss
Original Airdate: November 17, 1994

Have a *friendly* Thanksgiving.

Strapped for funds, Rachel asks her boss Terry for a hundred-dollar advance on her salary: She wants to fly to Vail to meet her family for their Thanksgiving ski trip. He declines her proposal. It turns out that Jack and Judy Geller are going to Puerto Rico for Thanksgiving, so Monica offers to make a holiday dinner for everyone.

When Ross stops by Carol and Susan's place, Susan informs him that she and Carol talk to the unborn baby. A little jealous, Ross asks if they speak about him. She says they do, but that they refer to Ross as "Bobo the Sperm Guy."

> ### A MATTER OF FAITH
>
> According to *Friends'* executive producer and creator Marta Kauffman, Mr. Geller is Jewish, but Mrs. Geller isn't.

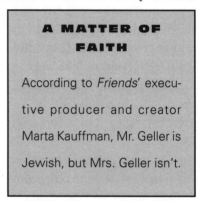

No doubt rebounding from his lost gig as Pacino's butt, Joey's excited to get a job modeling for posters for the City Free Clinic.

Rachel's depressed by the fact that she can't raise the money for her trip, until the gang thoughtfully chips in and buys her a plane ticket. Chandler shares with everyone why he hates the holiday: When he was nine his parents informed him on Thanksgiving during pumpkin pie that they were getting divorced. "It's very difficult to enjoy Thanksgiving dinner once you've seen it in reverse," he explains.

Later, Joey's in the subway and spots a woman who sells Obsession at Macy's—he was the Aramis Guy. He's on the verge of making a love connection when she sees something and suddenly runs off. Then Joey sees what she's seen—his face on a giant public service poster that reads, "What Mario Isn't Telling You . . . You Never Know Who Might Have VD." This poster turns out to be plastered all over the city. Joey's family thinks he has VD, so he too opts to have Thanksgiving at Monica's.

At Carol and Susan's place, Ross gets close to Carol's stomach and talks to the baby about a variety of topics, including his decision to major in paleontology. As Ross prenatally bonds, the baby kicks for the first time. Excitedly,

Ross sings The Monkees' theme to the baby with new lyrics including, "Hey, hey, I'm your daddy/ I'm the one without any breasts."

Before dinner, Chandler rushes in with news that the Underdog float has broken free from the Macy's parade over Washington Square Park. They all rush to the roof and get locked out. By the time the gang gets back into the apartment, the meal's burned and Rachel's missed her flight.

A THANKSGIVING TO REMEMBER: Monica displays her kitchen prowess in "The One Where Underdog Gets Away"

A little later the group's mood is lifted by the fact that Ugly Naked Guy is having Thanksgiving dinner with Ugly Naked Girl. Moved by the holiday spirit, they feast thankfully on grilled cheese sandwiches.

HEY, HEY, I'M YOUR DADDY: Ross croons to his unborn son in "The One Where Underdog Gets Away"

THE ONE WITH THE MONKEY

Director: Peter Bonerz
Writers: Adam Chase & Ira Ungerleider
Original Airdate: December 15, 1994

The monkey business begins.

It's still the holiday season and Marcel makes his big entrance. Ross' friend Bethel rescued the creature from a lab. "Hey, that monkey's got a Ross on its ass," says Chandler. Throughout the episode, Ross attempts to establish a bond with his new simian pal, who proves to be a little elusive. "He's just phoning it in," Ross says at one point of Marcel.

MONKEY BUSINESS

"'If Monkey were human, she'd be Meryl Streep,' says her proud trainer, Nerissa Politzer." —Some fulsome praise for the acting giant who plays Marcel, from an admittedly subjective source in *People*, April 10, 1995

Joey is unhappy to lose out on the seasonal department store Santa role and settles for being one of the helpers instead.

The gang makes a pact to remain dateless on New Year's Eve. To really get the holiday spirit going, nonriot grrrl Phoebe performs a series of extremely depressing songs at Central Perk. She admonishes two guys in the audience who are talking during her set. One of them turns out to be David (Hank Azaria), a charming physicist who was in the process of telling his friend Max that Phoebe's the most beautiful woman he has ever seen in his life.

Soon Phoebe and Max are dating, and she wants to break the no-date pact for New Year's Eve. Chandler then confesses that he has already asked out Janice. Right before New Year's, Monica confesses she's invited "Fun Bobby," an upbeat old boyfriend. Rachel and Joey admit to having invited dates too. Rachel's asked Paolo, and Joey has invited Sandy, an attractive single mother he met in a store. Ross is none too thrilled to be the only dateless friend.

A frustrated Phoebe provokes the shy David into giving her their first kiss while they're in his laboratory. Later David's partner Max comes into the coffeehouse with news that he and David have just gotten a grant so they can go do work in Minsk for three years. Before long, Max becomes furious because David doesn't want to go and leave behind his new love interest Phoebe.

At the New Year's Eve party, Janice clings closely to Chandler, while Joey's date Sandy arrives with her two children in tow. Paolo has missed his flight, but Fun Bobby does arrive. Sadly, his grandfather just died so he's not too much fun. Chandler breaks up with Janice again. Max bitterly calls Phoebe "Yoko," and says he's going alone to Minsk. Selflessly, Phoebe encourages David to go pursue his work.

By party's end, Joey's date Sandy is making out with Max. "It looks like that no-date pact thing worked out," Joey wisely points out. The friends anxiously discuss who can kiss who at midnight. Chandler is especially adamant that *someone* kiss him, so right at the stroke of midnight Joey memorably obliges.

Note: Peter Bonerz, who directed "The One with the Monkey," is a famous TV friend in his own right, having played Bob's dentist pal Dr. Jerry Robinson on *The Bob Newhart Show*.

Director: James Burrows
Writer: Alexa Junge
Original Airdate: January 5, 1995

While You Were Sleeping and *The Graduate* have nothing on "The One with Mrs. Bing."

WHILE HE WAS SLEEPING: Mr. Right is comatose—at least that's the way it turns out for Monica and Phoebe in "The One with Mrs. Bing"

At a sidewalk newsstand, Monica and Phoebe spy a very handsome man. Both of them seem intrigued with this guy, and as he walks away, Monica uncharacteristically whistles at him. This gets the fellow's attention—in fact, he stops in the middle of the street where he gets hit by an ambulance.

At the hospital, both women dote on their dashing coma guy. While he's sleeping, they imagine him as the ideal man. Before long a competition for his comatose attentions develops to the background theme of Mary Wells' "My Guy."

At Rachel and Monica's apartment, the whole gang and Paolo watch as Chandler's mother Nora Tyler (Morgan Fairchild) appears on *The Tonight Show with Jay Leno*. She's a sexy romance writer whose works include the seminal *Mistress Bitch*. She's promoting her latest tome, *Euphoria Unbound*. Mom's sultry persona and banter mortifies Chandler. Nora even tells the viewing audience that she bought her son his first condoms.

When she gets to town, Nora and the gang—plus Paolo—go to a Mexican restaurant. Rachel and Paolo's coziness drives Ross to drink. In the rest room area, Nora comforts the visibly upset Ross, and the two end up sharing a romantic kiss before Joey happens upon them.

The next morning Joey expresses his outrage at Ross breaking "the code." After some deliberation, Ross confesses his indiscretion to Chandler, who's very hurt. Chandler's also angry at Joey for not telling him right away about what he saw. Meanwhile, inspired by her literary hero Nora, Rachel decides

MOTHER AND CHILD REUNION: Chandler and his sexy mom Nora (Morgan Fairchild) share some quality prime time in "The One with Mrs. Bing"

to go to work on her first novel, to be titled *A Woman Undone*. From a brief reading, it's racy, atrocious stuff.

Chandler has a hard time forgiving "mother-kisser" Ross. He expects such behavior from his mother—"She's always been a Freudian nightmare," he explains— but not from his friend Ross.

Coma Guy finally comes out of it. To Monica and Phoebe's chagrin, he doesn't appreciate at all what they've both done for him.

Back at his apartment, Chandler finally confronts his mother about her behavior before she shuffles off sexily to Lisbon. "You kissed my best Ross!" he tells her forcefully. And having finally gotten things off his chest, Chandler forgives Ross and all is well again.

FRIENDLY FIRE: An outraged Joey confronts "mother-kisser" Ross in "The One with Mrs. Bing"

THE ONE WITH THE DOZEN LASAGNAS

Director: Paul Lazarus
Writers: Jeffrey Astrof & Mike Sikowitz and Adam Chase & Ira Ungerleider
Original Airdate: January 12, 1995

"The One with the Dozen Lasagnas" kicks off with one of *Friends'* TV moments. While sitting around together at Central Perk, the friends spontaneously sing a rousing rendition of *The Odd Couple* theme. Unwisely, Ross tries to transition into *I Dream of Jeannie*, but it's no go.

Monica has made a dozen lasagnas at the request of her Aunt Syl, but it turns out Syl wanted vegetarian. And so it is that Monica gets stuck with a dozen extra meat lasagnas that she will spend the rest of this tasty episode handing out.

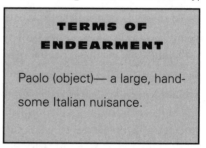

TERMS OF ENDEARMENT

Paolo (object)— a large, handsome Italian nuisance.

STRANGE BUT TRUE FRIENDS FACTS

Sometime during the first season, both Monica and Rachel and Chandler and Joey appear to have very quietly moved up a few floors in the apartment building.

Newly coupled Rachel and Paolo appear all lovey dovey, and they're about to head off to the Poconos for their first weekend away together. A distraught Ross considers calling Immigration on Paolo. Fortunately, the expectant dad finds some distraction by reading up on fatherhood.

An era ends when Joey and Chandler's kitchen table finally collapses. After some emotional debate, Joey and Chandler decide to commit to buying a new table together. It seems Chandler had a painful experience with his last roommate Kip: They bought a hibachi together, then Kip ran off and got married, the bastard. After much shopping, Chandler and Joey buy a foosball table as their new kitchen table. Monica turns out to be a total fooseball pro.

Ross—meat lasagna in hand—goes to Carol and Susan's apartment, knowing full well that Susan's a vegetarian. The women have Carol's amnio results, but Ross makes it clear that he doesn't want to know the sex of the baby.

Paolo pays a surprise visit to Phoebe at her massage cubicle, and proceeds to hit on her in the international language of lust. After softening the blow by baking Rachel the best oatmeal raisin cookie in the world, Phoebe tells her friend about the Italian's failed seduction attempt.

Rachel breaks up with Paolo on the balcony, and dumps the clothes from his suitcase off the roof. Politely and practically, Monica nonetheless gives Paolo a lasagna as a parting gift.

Not wanting to waste this opportunity, Ross tries to comfort Rachel and maybe make his move. "I don't even want to *think* about another guy," Rachel tells him. Then she casually and unintentionally breaks the big news to Ross that his child is going to be a boy.

THE ONE WITH THE BOOBIES

Director: Alan Myerson
Writer: Alexa Junge
Original Airdate: January 19, 1995

Finally, a little nudity among *Friends*. Chandler wanders into the girls' place one morning, and accidentally happens upon Rachel getting out of the shower. She grabs an afghan from the couch to cover herself and yells at him for violating her privacy. Always the gentleman, Chandler points out "that's a relatively open weave, and I can still see your, uh . . . nippular areas."

Later at the coffeehouse, the gang meets Phoebe's brand-new love interest, Roger (Fisher Stevens). Almost immediately Roger—who's a shrink—starts offering his professional opinion of all the friends. His comments are nearly as insightful as they are annoying.

Joey enters Central Perk with his father, Joey Sr. (Robert Costanzo). While his dad stays with him in the city, Joey's upset to find out that for the past six years his father has been having an affair with Ronni Rappelano, a pet mortician. Ronni turns up at the guys' apartment. Joey insists the aging love birds stay so that he can keep his eye on them.

Rachel remains upset that Chandler saw her "boobies" and that he continues to stare at her now-covered breasts. Ross suggests that they must do the adult thing to get past this awkwardness—the only mature thing is for Chandler to show her his "pee-pee." Rachel goes over to the guys' place to see Chandler's pee-pee, but accidentally opens the shower to see Joey's instead.

Roger's group analysis of the gang continues, and he continues to annoy virtually everyone in sight. Still, Roger seems to know what he's talking about. He's so good that Rachel opens up to him and discusses her deep feelings about the Weebles. Finally, the friends let Phoebe know that they hate Roger.

At first she thinks they feel this way because he's *too* perceptive. Chandler disagrees and explains that they just hate the guy.

Joey's mother, Gloria Tribbiani (Brenda Vaccaro), shows up at Joey and Chandler's place. She's mad at her son for convincing Joey Sr. to fess up, thus spoiling their mutually satisfactory marital arrangement. "I mean, it's nice," says Gloria of her hubby's affair. "He has a hobby."

> **TERMS OF ENDEARMENT**
>
> Tat (noun) — the male erogenous zone, as when Rachel demands to see tit for tat, Chandler says, "Well, I'm not showing you my tat."
>
> Nipular region (phrase) — more briefly, breasts, i.e., Rachel's topographical area viewed accidentally by Chandler in "The One with the Boobies."

Phoebe delicately breaks the news to Roger about her friends having a "liking" problem regarding him. Roger loses his cool and launches into a harsh critique of the gang's "dysfunctional group dynamic." Later, Phoebe announces that she's broken up with Roger. "And in some ways, I think he's so right for me," she explains. "It's just ... I hate that guy."

Joey sets off to get revenge and see Rachel in the shower, and accidentally sees Monica instead. "Sorry. Wrong boobies," he tells her. Later that day Monica goes over to surprise Joey in the shower and instead encounters his naked father. Interestingly, Joey's horny pop appears more than happy to see Monica.

THE ONE WITH THE CANDY HEARTS

Director: James Burrows
Writer: Billy Lawrence
Original Airdate: February 9, 1995

What could be more romantic than Valentine's Day with *Friends*? A lot, as it turns out.

While passing the time at Central Perk, Chandler and Joey encourage Ross to ask out Kristen (Heather Medway), a woman from his building who's also there. Valentine's Day is the next day and Phoebe briefly considers letting creepy Roger take her out. Joey and Chandler's Valentine's Day plans depend on a double date that the night before Joey convinced Chandler to go on.

At the restaurant that night, Chandler's less than thrilled to discover that the friend of Joey's date Lorraine (Nancy Valen) is the dreaded Janice, who he's already dumped two times in the previous five months. Before long, Joey and his date Lorraine get hot and bothered and leave Chandler behind with the needy, embittered Janice. The good news is that Joey leaves his credit card, which Chandler decides to utilize in style by ordering some pricey champagne. And so it is—in a powerful display of the destructive powers of alcohol—that Chandler wakes up in bed the next morning with Janice.

Back at Monica and Rachel's apartment, the women discuss creepy old boyfriends. Phoebe speaks of Pete Carney—a.k.a. Pete the Weeper—who used to cry every time they had sex. Monica mentions Howard, the "I Win" guy, who screamed that victorious phrase at the height of their passion. The women plan a cleansing ritual for Valentine's Day—a boyfriend bonfire.

At a Benihana-type hibachi restaurant on Valentine's Day, Ross and Kristen are on a date when lo and behold Carol and Susan are seated at the same table. Before long Susan's beeper goes off and she must leave. Carol's now left alone for Valentine's Day dinner, and a distracted Ross starts to ignore his date. He invites Carol to join them and in the process ruins his first date in nine years. Ross asks Carol to give their relationship another shot, and they share a nice kiss. They clearly still love each other on some level, but it's still a sexual no go. Carol tells him that he just needs to find the right woman, something Ross points out *she's* already done.

Standing around a smoking trash can, Monica, Rachel, and Phoebe gather piles of old boyfriend memorabilia. Rachel brings Barry's letters, Adam Ritter's boxers, and Paolo's grappa. Phoebe has the receipt from her dinner with someone named Nokululeoh. Monica has a picture of the hairy, naked Scotty Jarad. All the female bonding is cut short when the grappa makes the whole mess explode into a burst of flames. Three firemen arrive on the scene to deal with the boyfriend bonfire—it turns out they've already put out three others tonight.

At the coffeehouse, Janice brings Chandler a candy heart that says "Chan and Jan 4ever." Nonetheless he breaks up with her again, though this time she doesn't seem to believe him. "Don't you know it yet?" she asks him. "You love me, Chandler Bing."

The women make dates with the handsome firemen, who we discover are all married. Apparently, that ritual cleansing may not have worked after all.

THE ONE WITH THE STONED GUY

Director: Alan Myerson
Writers: Jeff Greenstein & Jeff Strauss
Original Airdate: February 16, 1995

Career opportunities and the high life converge in "The One with the Stoned Guy." Chandler's boss, "Big" Al Kostelic, wants to promote him to processing supervisor. So Chandler quits. He's been at this temp job for five years. "If I took this promotion, it'd be like admitting that this is what I actually do," he explains. He says he doesn't want to be another working stiff worrying about the WENUS—the Weekly Estimated Net Usage System, of course.

Helpfully, Phoebe tells Chandler about one of her massage clients, who's opening a new restaurant and needs a chef—a job that understandably interests Monica considerably more. Chandler, on the other hand, goes to meet with a career counselor. He's upset to find that according to this expert he's perfectly suited to a career in data processing—exactly what he's been doing.

THE MEDIUM IS THE MASSAGE: Phoebe hard at work pressing the flesh in "The One with the Stoned Guy"

Ross has a date with Celia (Melora Hardin), a.k.a. the Bug Lady. She's a comely curator of insects at the museum. The guys tell Ross that having the monkey with him will help him score, but instead Marcel and Celia battle it out. But Celia nonetheless comes over to Ross' pad again, and things get hot and heavy until she begs Ross to talk dirty. Feeling pressured, he says the mood-killing word "vulva." The next day Joey tries to coach Ross in how to more successfully talk dirty. While the buddies playact their smutty conversation, Chandler walks in and silently observes them to his great amusement.

TERMS OF ENDEARMENT

Tartlet (noun)— not a small sexy actress, but a luscious salmon dish prepared by Monica in "The One with the Stoned Guy."

Slap My Ass and Call Me Judy! (phrase)— a joyous exclamation by Steve (Jon Lovitz), who's one toke over the line in "The One with the Stoned Guy."

MALE BONDAGE: The boys hang out again in "The One with the Stoned Guy"

THE HIGH LIFE: Steve (Jon Lovitz) has a bad case of the munchies, which ruins Monica's big night of haute cuisine in "The One with the Stoned Guy"

Chandler decides to reenter the workplace when Big Al finally makes him an offer he can't refuse. Phoebe supportively stops by to visit Chandler in his new roomy window office and is much impressed by her friend's new clout.

For her culinary audition, Monica cooks up a storm. Monica's waitress pal Wendy backs out at the last moment, and Rachel— offended that she wasn't asked in the first place—finally agrees to help her out. Unfortunately, the restaurant's owner, Steve (Jon Lovitz), has smoked a joint on the way over and has a bad case of the munchies. The dinner turns into a mess because of Steve's stoned behavior. In retaliation, Phoebe gives Steve a rigorous and painful massage.

Note: Jon Lovitz, formerly of *Saturday Night Live*, encouraged Lisa Kudrow early on to pursue her career in performing.

THE ONE WITH TWO PARTS, PART ONE

Director: Michael Lembeck
Writers: David Crane & Marta Kauffman
Original Airdate: February 23, 1995

Let the NBC-bonding begin.

Chandler and Joey stop by Riff's—the familiar *Mad About You* dining spot—and encounter Ursula, Phoebe's identical twin sister who's a spacey waitress there. Apparently the sisters haven't talked in years.

Ross—who's dealing with a monkey who's acting out—goes off to Lamaze class with Carol and Susan. Ross has a little trouble explaining their unique family dynamic to the rest of the group. Later Ross actually ends up taking a Lamaze class with just Susan. At a subsequent Lamaze class, Carol has an anxiety attack about this whole childbirth thing.

At the office, Chandler calls in employee Nina Bookbinder (Jennifer Grant), who it seems has been throwing his WENUS out of whack. "I wouldn't want to do anything to hurt your WENUS," she tells him sweetly. Soon, though, the mood is broken when Chandler's superior Mr. Douglas (Dorien Wilson) reports that the company's ANUS—Annual Net Usage Statistics—is in. "It's pretty ugly," he says, "we haven't seen an ANUS this bad since the seventies." He tells Chandler that there will be cuts in every department. Chandler's ordered to lay off Nina. He tries but instead he starts dating her.

The defiant Marcel grabs the remote control at the girls' apartment and turns on *Family Matters*. Then he hits another button and somehow gets the TV stuck in Spanish mode. The friends sit back and watch an episode of *Laverne y Shirley*. Other shows they see *en español* include *The Waltons* and *The Patty Duke Show*.

Joey reports that he's become romantically interested in Ursula. He asks Phoebe's permission to ask her sister out. Phoebe acts increasingly uncomfortable with this idea. Growing up, Ursula stole her Thermos.

Friends' network neighbors Jamie (Helen Hunt) and Fran (Leila Kenzle) from *Mad About You* stop by Central Perk. Mistaking Phoebe for her sister, Jamie says, "This could be God's way of telling us, 'Eat at home.' "

Mr. Douglas wants to know why Chandler has not yet fired Nina. Trying to cover, he claims he already did but that she's crazy. At work, Nina soon becomes suspicious of why people are treating her as if she's mentally ill. Chandler tells her it's because they're jealous and promises her a big raise.

As his cover-up falls apart, Chandler proposes marriage. Offscreen he finally tells Nina the truth and she takes it pretty well, except for stapling his hand.

The other women convince Phoebe to tell Joey that she's uncomfortable with him dating Ursula before things get too serious between them. But when she knocks on Joey's door, Ursula answers wearing only Joey's shirt.

All episode, Monica's encouraging Rachel to finally take down the Christmas lights. When she finally does get around to it, she falls off the balcony.

Note: *One Day at a Time* types will recall that director Michael Lembeck played the husband to Julie Cooper (Mackenzie Phillips) on that series. Also, Jennifer Grant—who plays Nina Bookbinder—is the daughter of Dyan Cannon and Cary Grant, and is` familiar for her work on *Beverly Hills 90210*.

A FRIENDLY KISS: Phoebe—who's imitating her sister Ursula—provides lip service for Joey in "The One with Two Parts, Part Two"

THE MISSING PARTY: Joey fails to show at Phoebe's birthday bash in "The One with Two Parts, Part Two"

THE ONE WITH TWO PARTS, PART TWO

Director: Michael Lembeck
Writers: David Crane & Marta Kauffman
Original Airdate: February 23, 1995

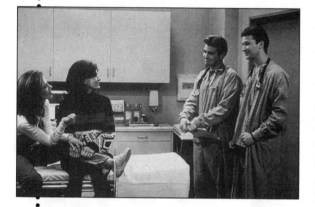

MUST SEE TV: The good doctors of NBC's *ER* show up a little early in "The One with Two Parts, Part Two"

The network continues in the second part of this historic double-header.

Part two opens with Rachel in the hospital admissions area after her fall. Somehow Rachel—who has no insurance—convinces the usually responsible Monica to engage in a little friendly insurance fraud by allowing Rachel to claim that *she's* Monica. While hanging at the hospital, Monica and doctor-loving Rachel also encounter the very friendly Dr. Rosen (*ER*'s Noah Wyle) and Dr. Mitchell (*ER*'s George Clooney). After some brief flirting, these awfully familiar emergency room doctors ask the women out. The women agree, and decide to trade identities to avoid being caught in their lie.

At Central Perk, Ross tells the guys about a dream that reveals his anxiety regarding his impending fatherhood. Later, Ross and his own father go to lunch and Jack Geller attempts, albeit awkwardly, to be supportive of his son. He tells him of his memory of Ross grabbing his finger in the hospital shortly after he was born.

Joey takes Ursula out for her birthday, having somehow forgotten that the same night's also her twin Phoebe's big surprise birthday party. Upon walking in the door at her party, Phoebe quickly scans the crowded apartment of friends and notices the conspicuous absence of Joey.

The good doctors arrive with wine "from the cellars of Ernest and Tova Borgnine" in hand. Monica and Rachel's big switch becomes an escalating comedy of errors, as the women trade insults using the wrong identities—i.e., Rachel tells the doctors, "By the way, in high school, I was a cow," or Monica explaining, "I used to wet my bed." Things get a tad uncomfortable for the doctors, who nervously compliment Monica's hummus. "God bless the chick-pea," Dr. Mitchell says. When Rachel's father calls, Monica takes advantage of her new identity to tattle that during Christmas break freshman year the *real* Rachel had sex with Billy Dreskin on her dad's bed.

The next day the whole gang's playing Scrabble—Monica puts down the word "TUSHIE." Chandler and Ross are back at the girls' place playing Scrabble, but Ross' "KIDNEY" becomes "IDNEY" when Marcel eats the "K" tile. They rush their simian friend to the hospital. At the hospital, Dr. Mitchell finds not only the "K" tile inside Marcel, but also an "M" and an "O." As Chandler explains, "We think he was trying to spell 'MONKEY.'" When Marcel wakes up postsurgery, he grabs Ross' finger—it's a movingly paternal moment for this nervous father-to-be.

Joey's upset because Ursula blows him off. On his behalf, Phoebe goes to Riff's to see her sister and they have a doubly spacey conversation. To soften the blow for him, Phoebe impersonates her sister and goes to the coffeehouse to talk Joey through the breakup. As Ursula, she asks if Joey would be willing to stop being friends with Phoebe if she said so. A good friend at heart, Joey flatly rejects this notion. Joey tells her she never looked more beautiful and they kiss—it's passionate, a rare display of passion among our pals. When Phoebe says "Wow," Joey realizes that it's actually her.

In a nicely multicultural moment, the episode ends with the gang at Monica and Rachel's apartment, speaking in Spanish translation, eating Chinese food, and noticing that Ugly Naked Guy's got a hula hoop.

MONKEYING AROUND: With a guilty-looking Marcel observing, the gang plays a little Scrabble in "The One with Two Parts, Part Two"

A FRIENDLY FRAUD: Monica and Rachel are summoned back to the scene of their crime in "The One with Two Parts, Part Two"

THE ONE WITH ALL THE POKER

Director: James Burrows
Writers: Jeffrey Astrof & Mike Sikowitz
Original Airdate: March 3, 1995

The games people play is one theme of "The One with All the Poker."

Whistling while they work, our gang helps Rachel send out résumés to, among other places, *Popular Mechanics* magazine.

Chandler inquires why Ross hasn't gone out with Linda again. "Is it still about her whole '*The Flintstones* could've really happened' thing?" Chandler—knowing who Ross is *really* hung up on—refers to his crush on Rachel. "Could you want her more?" Chandler asks. "Who?" Ross answers disingenuously. "Dee, the sarcastic sister from *What's Happening!!*" is Chandler's characteristically wiseass reply.

Later, when all the men are hanging out at Ross' apartment, Marcel puts on his favorite rock and roll oldie on the CD player—"The Lion Sleeps Tonight."

The women hear about the guys having a poker game and ask to be taught how to play. The gang's game turns into a mess. As Ross explains, "Phoebe gave away two jacks 'cause they didn't look happy." Indeed, for Phoebe, poker proves especially elusive. "And what is 'bluffing'? Is it not another word for . . . 'lying'!?" Subsequently, in an attempt to get a crash course in the card game, Monica's Aunt Iris (Beverly Garland) comes over to teach the women how to really play poker. Still, the guys win handily in the next poker game at Ross' place.

Rachel's thrilled when she gets a job interview at Saks Fifth Avenue. "It's like the mother ship is calling you home," Phoebe tells her. Afterward, an excited Rachel tells her pals that she had a great interview.

There's a poker rematch at the girls' place and Rachel seems to have finally gotten the knack. During the game, a phone call comes for Rachel informing her that she didn't get the Saks job. Rachel reacts by raising the stakes. The whole thing builds to one very expensive hand between Rachel and Ross. As it turns out, Rachel has a full house, and Ross claims defeat, but we'll never really know. Suspecting Ross has thrown the hand to buoy Rachel's spirits, Chandler and Joey lunge for the cards.

This fun-filled episode ends with everyone playing Pictionary—inexplicably, Joey guesses "The Unbearable Lightness of Being" from a vague drawing of a bean.

Note: Beverly Garland—who appears as the women's poker tutor Aunt Iris—is perhaps best known for playing the second wife on *My Three Sons*.

THE ONE WHERE THE MONKEY GETS AWAY

Director: Peter Bonerz
Writers: Jeffrey Astrof & Mike Sikowitz
Original Airdate: March 9, 1995

Reading the country-club newsletter sent by her mother—who sends the engagement notices to her daughter for "inspiration"—Rachel learns that her former fiancé, Barry, is marrying her onetime maid of honor, Mindy.

We discover that Ross and Marcel are doing great together—Ross is proud to report that Marcel's even learned the crucial difference between requests to "bring me the . . ." and "pee in the . . ." As far as things with Rachel go, there's less progress to report. At a pizza parlor, Ross tells the guys that he's finally going to let her know how he feels tonight, after she's spent all day caring for his monkey. "I can't remember the last time I got a girl to take care of my monkey," Chandler explains wistfully.

Under Rachel's watch, Marcel poops in Monica's shoe. While she's disposing of said poop—wrapped significantly in Barry and Mindy's engagement notice—Marcel escapes the apartment and makes a run for it. Before Ross turns up to discover this state of affairs, the rest of the gang frantically tries to find Marcel. This effort fails and finally Rachel breaks the bad news to Ross.

Unsurprisingly, Ross gets upset, particularly when Rachel tells him that she's already called Animal Control. He informs her that because Marcel is an illegal exotic animal, he's not allowed to have his beloved monkey in the city. Luisa Gianetti (Megan Cavanagh) arrives from Animal Control, and it turns out she's an old Lincoln High classmate of Monica's and Rachel's. She sat behind them in homeroom. They try to use this shared history to get Luisa to cut them some slack. No go. Apparently Rachel—who was prom queen, homecoming queen, and class president—had no time for this tomboyish woman back at Lincoln. Luisa's less resentful of Monica, she reports, who she said was overweight then and had problems of her own. "Would it have been so hard to say 'Mornin', Luisa,' or 'Nice overalls, Luisa'?" she asks emotionally. "You had to

MR. HECKLES R.I.P.

Sure he wasn't perfect, and yes, he did put Marcel in a dress. But still he was a memorable part of *Friends*. Heckles, we hardly knew ye.

be a bitch in high school," Ross tells Rachel, "you couldn't have been fat."

As they search the building for Marcel, Chandler and Joey are nearly diverted by two sexy neighbors. Finally, Phoebe and Monica spot Marcel in the boiler room. As Luisa fires her tranquilizer gun, Phoebe bravely dives in front of the monkey and takes the tranquilizer dart herself. In the confusion, Marcel scampers off until oddball neighbor Mr. Heckles traps him with a banana.

Ross and Rachel argue about the situation until the sight of a grocery delivery guy carrying bananas tips them off that Mr. Heckles has Marcel in his apartment. By the time they discover this, however, the nasty Heckles has already put Marcel in a dress and claims he's Patty the Monkey. By threatening to turn Luisa in for shooting Phoebe, the gang gets Luisa to back off about confiscating Marcel.

Later that night, Ross and Rachel make up, and things start to get quite cozy between them when from out of nowhere Rachel's fiancé Barry (Mitchell Whitfield) bursts in to tell Rachel that he's still in love with her.

THE ONE WITH THE EVIL ORTHODONTIST

Director: Peter Bonerz
Writer: Doty Abrams
Original Airdate: April 6, 1995

"The One with the Evil Orthodontist" begins with a timeless and important debate. While the friends are arguing over whether they'd rather be Mr. Peanut or Mr. Salty, Monica notices someone with a telescope looking at them. "I feel violated," says Chandler, "and not in a good way." Then Phoebe notices that Ugly Naked Guy's gotten gravity boots, and they all rush to spy on him.

Chandler reports that he's had a dream date with a woman named Danielle, but he wonders how long to wait before calling her back.

Rachel and Barry meanwhile are spotted looking cozy outside Central Perk. They've gone to the Russian Tea Room for lunch, then Bendel's, and had a lovely time together. Ross, of course, is less than thrilled with this turn of events. Later Rachel goes to Barry's office to say good-bye to him once and for all. Instead, they end up making love in his dental chair. Rachel and Barry's post-coital discussion is interrupted by the arrival of a young patient. Ross is outraged when he hears about this dental visit.

Chandler practices the phone message he'll leave on Danielle's answering machine. After finally calling, he waits for Danielle to call him back. Instead there's an incoming call from Mindy (Jennifer Grey of *Dirty Dancing* fame), Rachel's former maid of honor, who's now engaged to Barry. Mindy wants to get together with Rachel the next day. At Central Perk they meet and Mindy asks Rachel to be *her* maid of honor. Mindy tells Rachel that she's suspicious that Barry's having an affair. Rachel comforts her by saying Barry acted odd when they were first engaged too. Mindy takes this chance to confess that she and Barry were having an affair back then.

The resourceful Joey tracks down the peeper's phone number. As it turns out, the peeper's a woman, and a very complimentary one who praises Joey's physical condition and passes along word that Monica looked like Ingrid Bergman in her green dress the other day. They are both charmed.

Rachel and Mindy go to Barry's office so they can both break up with him, but Mindy ends up forgiving the evil orthodontist. "Look, I know he's not perfect," she tells Rachel. "But the truth is . . . at the end of the day . . . I still really want to be Mrs. Dr. Barry Farber, DDS."

Later that night, the emotional Mr. Peanut discussion continues at Central Perk, with Phoebe explaining that he's gay. Before she can elaborate, Danielle enters. It seems that she's been trying to reach Chandler too. Unfortunately, the fact that Danielle went out of her way to find him strikes Chandler as being "needy." Groucho-like, Chandler is completely turned off by her display of interest in him.

FRIENDLY ANALYSIS

Sure we love *Friends*, but why? And how do we *feel* about that? Could it be that being the most nurturing show on the networks actually helps your Nielsen ratings? In search of some professional counseling on this topic, we talked—free of charge—to Dr. Marilyn Kagan, a popular psychotherapist on KFI Radio in Los Angeles, and more recently the host of her own television talk show.

How do you explain the Friends *phenomenon, psychologically speaking?*

It *is* a phenomenon. I guess the show's supposed to be for twentysomethings, but I think it hits all of us in a sense because these friends *are* like a substitute family. Especially when you're in your twenties, you're moving out of your parents' home and you haven't moved into a long-term relationship and started building your own family yet. That period of limbo between leaving our real families and the beginning of adulthood responsibilities is getting longer. So a lot of people probably depend on their friends more now than even ten or twenty years ago. I think there's some connection with feeling safe and getting a sense of unconditional love.

THE ONE WITH THE FAKE MONICA

Director: Gail Mancuso
Writers: Adam Chase & Ira Ungerleider
Original Airdate: April 27, 1995

Never has there been as friendly a case of credit card fraud as in "The One with the Fake Monica." Someone's gotten hold of Monica's credit card number and starts buying up a storm. Ever the control freak, Monica's aghast at the reckless purchases being made in her name. She obsesses on the great life this woman's leading on her credit card. "She's got everything I want," says the outraged and envious Monica. "And she *doesn't* have my mother!"

That randy Marcel has begun to hump everything from a lamp to Rachel's innocent Curious George doll. "Let's just say my Curious George doll is no longer curious," Rachel reports. The veterinarian tells Ross that Marcel's behavior is not a phase, and that he's going to have to give up his monkey pal. Supposedly Marcel needs the sort of monkey lovin' he can only get knocking around a zoo. In fatherly fashion, Ross says they're applying to a number of zoos, including one in San Diego and Miami—an institution Chandler dismisses as a total "party zoo."

At Central Perk, Joey searches for a new stage name. He rejects Chandler's suggestions until he jokingly offers up "Joseph Stalin." Unaware of the dictator of the same name, Joey *loves* it.

Monica goes to tap class to track down her credit card thief, and drags the other women with her. After a while, the fake Monica (Claudia Shear, star of the one-woman play *Blown Sideways Through Life*) arrives. The real Monica tells the fake one that her name's "Monana." Surprisingly, the fake Monica brings out a new, carefree side of the old one. Monica continues to go wild with her new pal, until the fake Monica is finally arrested.

Ross is upset because Marcel was rejected at Scranton, their "safety zoo."

Desperate, he meets at the coffeehouse with the slightly disreputable Dr. Baldharar (Harry Shearer), who seemingly wants the monkey for some sordid purposes. Fortunately, Joey and Chandler rush in with the thrilling news that Marcel has gotten into the San Diego Zoo.

Everyone but Monica goes to the airport to see Marcel off. During an emotional parting, Marcel starts humping Ross' leg.

The episode ends with Joey auditioning under his brand-new stage name, Holden McGroin.

Note: The auditioners seen in the shadows during the last scene are played by none other than *Friends'* own executive producers Marta Kauffman, Kevin S. Bright, and David Crane.

THE ONE WITH THE ICK FACTOR

Director: Robby Benson
Writer: Alexa Junge
Original Airdate: May 4, 1995

"The One with the Ick Factor" is an inspired, sexy episode for all ages.

Hanging out at Central Perk, Rachel discusses the dream she had last night in which she and Chandler had sex on the coffeehouse's table. Ross isn't pleased by this sharing, but Chandler's thrilled to hear that he was good. "'Cause in my own dreams, I'm surprisingly inadequate," he tells Rachel.

A FRIENDLY WORKPLACE: Pheebs does some temp work for Chandler in "The One with the Ick Factor"

Phoebe's looking for work until her massage business picks up, and Joey suggests that she work for Chandler, whose secretary will be out for a few weeks getting a breast reduction. At work, Chandler finds his fears confirmed that Phoebe's none too easy to work with. Phoebe also informs Chandler that everybody at work doesn't like him and that they even imitate his tendency to emphasize an unusual word when he speaks.

Monica heads off for a date with "young Ethan." She says he's a senior in college, and reluctantly admits she's told him she's twenty-two when in fact she's twenty-six. After their evening together, Monica asks Ethan (Stan Kirsch) to stay the night. Before they sleep together, Ethan confesses that he's actually a virgin. After sex, Monica confesses to her real age—"twenty-five and thirteen months." This leads Ethan to admit that he's really a senior in high school. Monica freaks out. He tells her that he's in love. She tells him, "You shouldn't even be here! It's—it's a school night! Oh my God, I'm like the women you see with shiny guys named Chad. I'm Joan Collins."

Meanwhile Ross keeps getting beeper messages for 55-JUMBO—a sex service—instead of 55-JIMBO, the line he keeps so he'll know when Carol goes into labor. As if that's not frustrating enough, Rachel tells of her new sexual dream which featured Chandler and Joey.

Chandler goes out with Phoebe and their coworkers for a night of karaoke and tries to win them over. Later, Phoebe explains to him that no matter what he's still the boss. And so it is that Chandler gives up on being Mister Nice Guy and begins to embrace the power of his position.

Ethan comes to Central Perk to talk things out with Monica. Her mature reason for not pursuing their relationship is "Ethan, it's . . . icky."

Later, Ross is hanging around the women's apartment when Rachel dozes off and has what's clearly a sex dream involving him. An ecstatic Ross breaks into a victory dance, and in doing so he slams into the side table and wakes up Rachel. Still, the air's thick with romantic possibility. Just then Ross' beeper goes off. Realizing his baby's on the way, Ross jumps over the couch and crashes down. Ross rushes the gang out to go to the hospital, then stands there in the stairwell overwhelmed by the moment. Lovingly, the friends lead him gently out of the building.

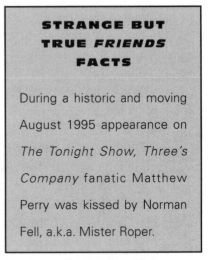

STRANGE BUT TRUE *FRIENDS* FACTS

During a historic and moving August 1995 appearance on *The Tonight Show, Three's Company* fanatic Matthew Perry was kissed by Norman Fell, a.k.a. Mister Roper.

Note: Director Robby Benson is also familiar as a young actor in films like *Ode to Billy Joe, Ice Castles,* and *One on One.*

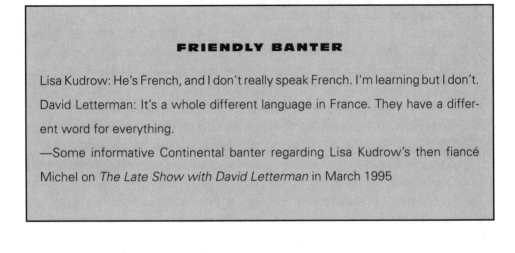

FRIENDLY BANTER

Lisa Kudrow: He's French, and I don't really speak French. I'm learning but I don't.

David Letterman: It's a whole different language in France. They have a different word for everything.

—Some informative Continental banter regarding Lisa Kudrow's then fiancé Michel on *The Late Show with David Letterman* in March 1995

THE ONE WITH THE BIRTH

Director: James Burrows
Writers: Teleplay by Jeff Greenstein & Jeff Strauss, Story by David
    Crane & Marta Kauffman
Original Airdate: May 11, 1995

With "The One with the Birth," the extended *Friends* family gets a little bigger.

The gang beats Susan and Carol to the maternity area. In the waiting room, Joey—who's watching the Knicks game—encounters Lydia (Leah Rimini), a pregnant Celtics fan. Since the father of the child isn't with her, Joey ends up sweetly attending to Lydia in the delivery room.

True to form, Rachel continues to flirt with Carol's obstetrician—Dr. Franzblau (Jonathan Silverman). Making note of her intense attraction to physicians, Chandler guesses—correctly, it turns out—that Rachel's father is a doctor.

Ross argues with Susan and Carol about the baby's name. They had agreed on "Jamie," but now say it'll be "Jordie" since Susan's first girlfriend was named Jamie. Because of their incessant fighting, Carol throws both Ross and Susan out of the delivery room. They keep right on feuding until Phoebe forces them into a utility closet to hash things out. Unfortunately, they all get locked in the tiny room. There Ross expresses his jealousy of Susan, and his frustration that *she* gets to go home with the baby. Susan points out that as a father he has a defined role. There's a Father's Day, but no Lesbian Lover's Day. Ross responds, "*Every* day is Lesbian Lover's Day!"

The tension continues until somehow Phoebe puts things in perspective by pointing out that the baby's lucky to have both of them love him so much.

She puts on the overalls she finds that have a name tag of someone named Ben. Pulling together to get out of the closet, they hoist Phoebe up to the air vent. Once she's on her way, a janitor comes by and finally lets them out.

Joey goes back to check on Lydia and the baby, but backs off when he see the real father has arrived.

Back in Carol's delivery room, Ross and Susan finally return shortly before the baby appears. Asked by Carol what the baby looks like, Ross says, "Kind of like my Uncle Ed covered in Jell-O."

Inspired by the name on the overalls, they decide to name the baby boy Ben. Remarkably, Ross and Carol have nearly bonded. "Susan, he looks just like you," Phoebe tells the proud auxiliary mom. "Hi, Ben," says a clearly moved Monica. "I'm your Aunt Monica. I—I will always have gum." That would be perfection, you can almost hear Ben say.

"The One with the Birth" ends with Ross assuring Ben that, though he won't always be around, he'll always be there for him.

Note: Jonathan Silverman, who plays Dr. Franzblau, is now playing "doctor" in a different way on the NBC series *The Single Guy*.

THE ONE WHERE RACHEL FINDS OUT

Director: Kevin S. Bright
Writer: Chris Brown
Original Airdate: May 18, 1995

Already a proud papa, Ross passes photos of Ben around to the gang at Central Perk.

Joey asks Chandler if he can borrow a little money, then explains that he'll be getting a cash infusion for helping out down at the N.Y.U. medical school with some research. Reluctantly, Joey explains that he's making a most intimate contribution to a fertility study, and getting seven hundred dollars for his trouble. "Wow!" says Phoebe, "you're going to make money hand over fist." There's a problem with this dream gig. Joey has met a new woman named Melanie (Corinne Bohrer), who really wants to have sex with him. "That crazy bitch," says a sympathetic Chandler. Joey points out that it's a sticky situation because he's not allowed to conduct any personal "experiments" until the program's over in another week. Joey discusses how he's going to deal with Melanie's sexual desires, and Monica suggests he just satisfy her, a concept that at first utterly eludes Joey.

Later that day, Ross stops by the women's apartment with a suitcase in hand. At the last minute, he must go to China for work. "It's a whole big bone thing," Ross explains helpfully. He's not happy to find out that Rachel's out for drinks with a fellow named Carl. Before rushing off, Ross leaves a birthday gift with Chandler to give to Rachel that evening.

TERMS OF ENDEARMENT

Mayor of the Zone (phrase)—Joey elected Ross to this office in "The One with the Blackout"— his charming way of informing Ross that he'd been in the Friend Zone too long to ask out Rachel.

That night the rest of the gang and Melanie are at Rachel's party, and Melanie talks about her fruit-basket business, the "Three Basketeers." Joey adds that it's "like the Three Musketeers only with fruit." Rachel opens her assorted gifts—including a fruit basket from Melanie, a Travel Scrabble game from Chandler, and a Dr. Seuss book entitled *Oh, the Places You'll Go* from Joey. "That book got me through some tough times," Joey says meaningfully. When they get to Ross' gift, Rachel's extremely moved.

He's given her an antique cameo pin they'd seen months ago that she told him reminded her of one that her grandmother once had.

In discussing Ross' thoughtfulness, Chandler accidentally clues Rachel into the world's worst kept secret—that Ross loves her. This is the *big* moment when Rachel finally finds out. "Does he, like, want to go out with me?" she asks. "Well, given that he's hopelessly in love with you, he probably wouldn't mind getting a cup of coffee or something," Joey tells her. Rachel rushes to the airport to catch Ross before he leaves. She just misses him, and gives a message for him to a stewardess. Unfortunately the stewardess gives it to the wrong passenger.

Later that night, Joey seems to have grasped Monica's suggestion and has convinced Melanie that he's the most unselfish lover in the world. "Boy, somebody's getting a *big* fruit basket tomorrow," Melanie tells him.

Meanwhile across the hall, Monica advocates on her brother's behalf with Rachel. When Rachel says finally that she's thinking that having a romantic relationship with Ross might be great, Monica adds, "Me too! We'd be like friends-in-law."

A week later, however, Rachel's changed her mind and decided "this whole Ross thing is not a good idea." But while having wine on the balcony with Carl (Tommy Blaze) as he yammers on about his pet peeve, Ed Begley, Jr., Rachel finds herself thinking about Ross. Suddenly an imaginary Ross appears and tells her he's been in love with her since the ninth grade. She expresses her fears, but fortunately the imaginary Ross becomes very smooth. He—unlike the real Ross—passionately kisses her. Finally knowing what she must do now, Rachel runs out on Carl to go to the airport. She arrives at the gate just in time to watch as Ross exits the plane with Julie (Lauren Tom), a new love interest he's met in China. We freeze on Rachel's smiling face just before she sees them.

Friendly Words

The Quotable *Friends*

Friends may be the most furiously verbal program in television history. If the art of conversation was nearing death, this chatty show may have very well single-handedly revived the sucker. Even during its relatively brief history, the show's talented writers have managed to offer witty and wise words on virtually any topic of interest. And so in this "Friendly Words" section, you'll find at least a partial sampling of some of the greatest lines from the show's first season archives, as divided by subject.

THE ONE ABOUT THE REAL WORLD

MONICA: Welcome to the real world. It sucks. You're gonna love it.
　　—Rachel's bittersweet greeting from her old pal in the pilot episode

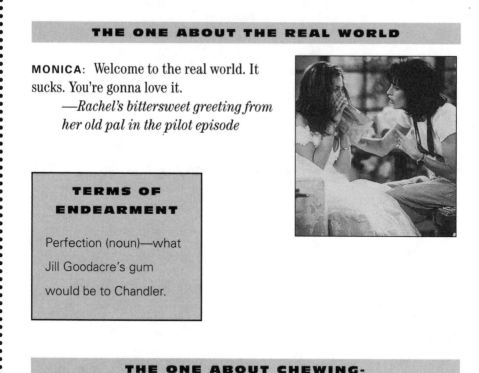

TERMS OF ENDEARMENT

Perfection (noun)—what Jill Goodacre's gum would be to Chandler.

THE ONE ABOUT CHEWING-GUM ETIQUETTE

CHANDLER (VOICE-OVER): What the hell was that? Mental note: If Jill Goodacre offers you gum, you take it. If she offers you a mangled animal carcass, you take it.
　　—Internal ATM thoughts in "The One with the Blackout"

THE ONE ABOUT CHEWING-GUM ETIQUETTE (PART TWO)

CHANDLER: You know, on second thought, gum would be perfection.
JILL GIVES CHANDLER AN ODD LOOK, AND A PIECE OF GUM.
CHANDLER (VOICE-OVER): (IN DISBELIEF) "Gum would be perfection"?? "Gum would be perfection"?? Could have said "gum would be nice" or "I'll have a stick." But, noooo. For me, gum is *perfection*. I loathe myself.
　　—Further Chandleresque self-flagellation in "The One with the Blackout"

THE ONE ABOUT AN IMMODEST PROPOSAL
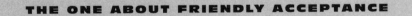

JOEY: Well, if you can't talk dirty to me, how are you going to talk dirty to her? Now tell me you want to caress my butt.

—*Joey tries to improve Ross' interpersonal communication skills in "The One with the Stoned Guy"*

THE ONE ABOUT FRIENDLY ACCEPTANCE
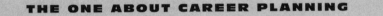

CHANDLER: It's okay. It's okay. I was always rooting for you two guys to get together.

—*Chandler's supportive reaction to seeing the above dirty talk in "The One with the Stoned Guy"*

THE ONE ABOUT CAREER PLANNING

RACHEL: I'm going to get one of those job things.

—*One ambitious woman decides to reenter—make that enter—the workplace in the pilot episode*

THE ONE ABOUT BEEPERS

RACHEL: What are you playing with?
ROSS: It's my new beeper.
JOEY: What the hell's a paleontologist need a beeper for?
MONICA: Is it for, like, dinosaur emergencies? "Help! Come quick! They're still extinct!"

—*An urgent question answered in "The One with the Ick Factor"*

THE ONE ABOUT DATING

MONICA: Okay, everybody. Relax. This is not even a date. It's just two people going out to dinner and not having sex.

CHANDLER: Sounds like a date to *me*.

—A tragically revealing exchange about the nineties dating game in the pilot episode

THE ONE ABOUT WEDDING ETIQUETTE

MONICA: Joey, stop hitting on her. It's her wedding day.

JOEY: What? Like there's some rule or something?

—Having flirted with runaway bride Rachel, Joey asks a reasonable question in the pilot episode

THE ONE ABOUT LESBIANISM

CHANDLER: Sometimes I wish I was a lesbian. Did I say that out loud?

—A true confession in the pilot episode

OPENING ACTS

"It was about five in the morning on the Warner Bros. lot," recalls Matthew Perry of the time he and the other cast members danced the night away for the cameras while filming that famous *Friends* opening sequence. "Now, I'm one of the worst dancers in the history of the world. And knowing full well that all my friends would make vicious fun of me, I still had to dance the whole time. The original opening of the show was just all of us dancing around that fountain. Then the network said that version looked like we were having too much fun and not letting the audience in on it. So they changed the opening by putting in some footage from the show."

THE ONE ABOUT FOLLOWING ONE'S BLISS

RACHEL: (WAVING A LETTER) I got an interview! I got an interview!
PHOEBE/MONICA: Oh my God! Where?
RACHEL: (WITH AWE) Saks. Fifth. Avenue.
MONICA: (HEARTFELT) Oh, Rachel.
PHOEBE: It's like the mother ship is calling you home.
—A heavenly moment in "The One with All the Poker"

THE ONE ABOUT CONFLICTING DESIRES

JOEY: Pheebs, you wanna help?
PHOEBE: Oh, I wish I could, but I really don't want to.
—An early Phoebian comment in the pilot episode

THE ONE ABOUT THE BOYFRIEND BONFIRE

PHOEBE: Okay, now we need the sage branches and the sacramental wine.
MONICA: All I have is oregano and a Fresca.
PHOEBE: That's okay. (CONSULTING PAPER) All right, now we need the semen of a righteous man.
RACHEL: Okay, Pheebs. You know what: If we had that, we wouldn't be doing the ritual here.
—The women mix up a potent brew in "The One with the Candy Hearts"

THE ONE ABOUT TAKING PRIDE IN ONE'S WORK

CHANDLER: All right, kids, I've got to get to work. If I don't input those numbers . . . it doesn't make much of a difference.
—An occupational realization in the pilot episode

THE ONE ABOUT UNIVERSALITY

RACHEL: Cool. "Urkel" in Spanish is "Urkel."
—*Rachel discovers it's a small world after all in "The One with Two Parts, Part One"*

THE ONE ABOUT INDEPENDENCE

MONICA: Come on. You can't live off your parents your whole life.
RACHEL: I know that! That's why I was getting married!
—*A revealing conversation between old friends in the pilot episode*

THE ONE ABOUT THE SINGLE WOMAN THEORY

ROSS: You know what the scariest part is? What if—what if there's only *one* woman for everybody? Ya know, what if you only get one woman and that's it? Unfortunately, in my case, there was only one woman for *her*.
—*Ross expresses a deep dark fear in the pilot episode*

THE ONE ABOUT TRUE LOVE AND HAPPY DAYS

RACHEL: (TO HERSELF) See, but Joanie *loved* Chachi. That's the difference.
—*Rachel realizing what was lacking in her relationship with orthodontist Barry in the pilot episode*

THE ONE ABOUT A FEW NOT-SO-GOOD MEN

MONICA: Is it me? Is it like I have a beacon that only dogs and men with severe emotional problems can hear?
—*A romantic cry for help in the pilot episode*

THE ONE ABOUT DATING LANGUAGE

MONICA: Uh, no. Loosely translated, "We should do this again" means "You will never see me naked."

RACHEL: Since when?

JOEY: Since always. It's like dating language. You know, like . . . "It's not you" means "It is you."

CHANDLER: Or "You're such a nice guy" means "I'm gonna be dating leather-wearing alcoholics and complaining about them to you."

PHOEBE: Or—or, you know, um . . . "I think we should see other people" means "Ha, ha . . . I already am."

RACHEL: And everybody knows this?

JOEY: Oh, yeah. It cushions the blow.
   —*A useful social primer in "The One with the Thumb"*

THE ONE ABOUT SPILLING THE BEANS

RACHEL: Does he, like, want to go out with me?

JOEY: Well, given that he's desperately in love with you, he probably wouldn't mind getting a cup of coffee or something.
   —*Rachel grapples with a brave new world after hearing about Ross' feelings for her in "The One Where Rachel Finds Out"*

THE ONE ABOUT ATHLETIC COMPETITION

CHANDLER: Yep, we sure showed those Hassidic jewelers a thing or two about softball.
   —*Savoring a rare win in "The One with the Thumb"*

THE ONE ABOUT THE SOCIAL CALENDAR

JOEY: So when are we gonna meet this guy?

MONICA: Hmm. Let's see, today's Monday . . . Never.
   —*In "The One with the Thumb"*

THE ONE ABOUT FRIENDS AND LOVERS

MONICA: Why should I let them meet him? I mean, I bring a guy home and within five minutes they're like coyotes picking off the weak members of the herd.

—In "The One with the Thumb"

THE ONE ABOUT KISSING

CHANDLER: Yeah. I think for us, kissing is pretty much an opening act. You know. I mean, it's like . . . the comedian you have to sit through before Pink Floyd comes out.

ROSS: And it's not that we don't like the comedian. It's just . . . that's not why we bought the ticket.

—The guys try to explain the role of lip service in the amorous arts in "The One with the Sonogram at the End"

THE ONE ABOUT THE IMPORTANCE OF BEING ALAN

MONICA: Can I ask you guys a question? Do you think that Alan's maybe . . . sometimes . . .

ROSS: What?

MONICA: I don't know . . . a little *too* . . . Alan?

RACHEL: No. That's impossible! No one can be *too* Alan.

ROSS: Yeah. It's his innate Alan-ness that we adore.

CHANDLER: I, personally, could have a gallon of Alan.

—In a generous moment, the friends praise one of Monica's love interests in "The One with the Thumb"

THE ONE ABOUT SMOKING

CHANDLER: Hey, you know, I have had it with you guys and your cancer and your emphysema and your heart disease. *The bottom line is smoking's cool and you know it.*

—An irresponsible point in "The One with the Thumb"

THE ONE ABOUT ASTUTE TV CRITICISM

CHANDLER: (RE: TV) Oh, I think this is the episode of *Three's Company* where there's some kind of misunderstanding.
—*A tongue-in-cheek critique in "The One with the Sonogram at the End"*

THE ONE ABOUT SIBLING RIVALRY

MONICA: As far as my parents are concerned, Ross can do no wrong. You see, he's the prince. Apparently, they had some big ceremony before I was born.
—*Ross' little sister comments on Mom and Dad always liking him better in "The One with the Sonogram at the End"*

THE ONE ABOUT SCARY SIGHTS

CHANDLER: Ugly Naked Guy got a Thighmaster.
THE OTHERS: Eeaagh!
—*An unseen yet still horrifying image in "The One with the Sonogram at the End"*

THE ONE ABOUT SIBLING RIVALRY (PART TWO)

MONICA: I know they say you can't change your parents. But, boy, if you could . . . (TO ROSS) I'd want *yours.*
—*A little sister's slightly jealous confession to her beloved older brother in "The One with the Sonogram at the End"*

THE ONE ABOUT PUSHY PARENTS

JACK: I'm not going to tell you what they spent on that wedding. But forty thousand dollars is a lot of money.
JUDY: Well, at least she had the chance to leave a man at the altar.
—*Those inimitable Gellers in "The One with the Sonogram at the End"*

THE ONE ABOUT CAREER WOMEN

PHOEBE: You know, it's worse when you're twins.

RACHEL: You're a twin?

PHOEBE: Oh, yeah. We don't speak. She's this real high-powered, driven career type.

CHANDLER: What does she do?

PHOEBE: She's a waitress.

> —*Phoebe talks about her slightly tense relationship with her sister Ursula in "The One with the Sonogram at the End"*

THE ONE ABOUT DENTISTRY

BARRY: A month ago I wanted to hurt you more than I've ever hurt anyone in my life. And I'm an orthodontist.

—*Rachel's ex makes an honest confession in "The One with the Sonogram at the End"*

THE ONE ABOUT BABY NAMES

SUSAN: (TO ROSS) Oh, please. What's wrong with "Helen"?

ROSS: "Helen Geller"? I don't think so.

> —*Two interested parties discuss the possibilities in "The One with the Sonogram at the End"*

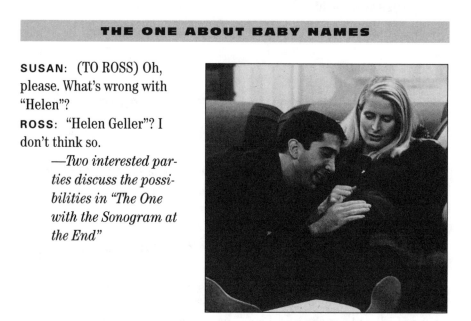

THE ONE ABOUT BABY NAMES (PART TWO)

CAROL: You're not actually suggesting "Helen Willick-Bunch-Geller"? 'Cause I think that borders on child abuse.
> —*A contrary view from the gender-bending mother-to-be in "The One with the East German Laundry Detergent"*

THE ONE ABOUT BREASTS

JOEY: You know what blows my mind? Women can see breasts anytime they want. Just look down, and there they are. How you get any work done is beyond me.
> —*One honest man's view in "The One with the East German Laundry Detergent"*

THE ONE ABOUT MALE DATING STRATEGY

JOEY: Why do you have to break up with her? Be a man. Just stop calling.
> —*Joey offers Chandler the easy way out in "The One with the East German Laundry Detergent"*

THE ONE ABOUT PARENTAL NAY-SAYING

MONICA: Did he give you the whole "You're not up to this" thing again?
RACHEL: Oh, yeah. I got the extended disco version. With three choruses of "You'll never make it on your own."
> —*The roommates commiserate in "The One with the East German Laundry Detergent"*

THE ONE ABOUT PARENTAL NAY-SAYING
(PART TWO)

MONICA: Mom already called this morning. Just to remind me not to wear my hair up. Did you know my ears are not my best feature?
ROSS: Some days it's all I can think about.

> —*A brother and sister chat in "The One Where Nana Dies Twice"*

THE ONE ABOUT SEDUCTION

JOEY: Come on. We were great together. And not just at the fun stuff. But, like, *talking*, too.

> —*A foolproof pickup line in "The One with the East German Laundry Detergent"*

THE ONE ABOUT MATCHMAKING FAUX PAS

JOEY: Monica. I'm telling you this guy is perfect for you!
MONICA: Forget it. Not after your cousin who could belch the alphabet.

> —*A bad date recalled in "The One with the East German Laundry Detergent"*

THE ONE ABOUT TOGETHERNESS

PHOEBE: This is nice. We never do anything just the two of us.
CHANDLER: That's great. Maybe tomorrow we can rent a car and run over some puppies.
PHOEBE: Eehh! I don't want to do that.

> —*Two friends enjoying a little time with each other in "The One with the East German Laundry Detergent"*

THE ONE ABOUT RAMBUNCTIOUSNESS

MONICA: Oh my God!

JOEY: What?

MONICA: Hello! Were we at the same table? It's like—it's like . . . cocktails in Appalachia!

JOEY: Come on. They're close.

MONICA: *Close??* She's got her tongue in his ear!

JOEY: Like you've never gotten a little rambunctious with Ross.

   —*Monica reacts to seeing the couple Joey's said are brother and sister making out in "The One with the East German Laundry Detergent"*

THE ONE ABOUT LAUNDRY AND WEIGHT LOSS

RACHEL: Uh . . . excuse me. We, uh, we had this cart.

HORRIBLE WOMAN: Yeah, well, I had a twenty-four-inch waist. You lose things. Outta my way.

   —*A tense, weighty exchange in "The One with the East German Laundry Detergent"*

THE ONE ABOUT HUGE MISUNDERSTANDINGS

MONICA: Joey. What would you do if you were omnipotent?

JOEY: I'd probably kill myself.

MONICA: Excuse me?

JOEY: Hey, if Little Joey's dead, then I got no reason to live.

ROSS: Uh, Joey. (ENUNCIATING) *Om*nipotent.

JOEY: You are? Ross, I'm sorry.

   —*A prickly bit of confusion in "The One with George Stephanopoulos"*

THE ONE ABOUT PONDERING THE LESBIAN LIFESTYLE

ROSS: You know what? I'd better pass on the game. I'm just gonna go home and think about my ex-wife and her lesbian lover.
JOEY: The hell with hockey. Let's *all* do that.
   —*Guy talk in "The One with George Stephanopoulos"*

THE ONE ABOUT TAXES

RACHEL: Isn't this exciting! I earned this. I wiped tables for it, I steamed milk for it, and it's—(OPENING IT)—not worth it. Who's FICA? Why is he getting my money?
   —*With her first Central Perk paycheck, certain harsh fiscal realities hit Rachel hard in "The One with George Stephanopoulos"*

THE ONE ABOUT THE MYTHIC PERFECT MAN

MONICA: Okay. He's a lawyer who teaches sculpting on the side. And he can *dance.*
PHOEBE: Oooo! And he's the kind of guy who, when you're talking, he's listening, you know, and not saying, "Yeah, I understand," but really wondering what you look like naked.
   —*Two dreamers share their vivid fantasy lives in "The One with Mrs. Bing"*

THE ONE ABOUT GREAT LITERATURE

RACHEL: Chandler, I've got to tell you, I love your mom's books. I love her books! I cannot get on a plane without one. This is so cool.
CHANDLER: Yeah, well, it's not so cool when you're eleven and all your friends are passing around page 79 of *Mistress Bitch.*
   —*A lively literary chat in "The One with Mrs. Bing"*

THE ONE ABOUT GREAT LITERATURE
(PART TWO)

NORA: Ross, listen to me. I have sold a hundred million copies of my books. You know why?

ROSS: The girl on the cover with her nipples showing?

> —*A reasonable guess in "The One with Mrs. Bing"*

THE ONE ABOUT MODERN MOTHERHOOD

NORA: (ON TV) Oh no. I'm a fabulous mom. I bought my son his first condoms.

> —*A very public disclosure made to Jay Leno in "The One with Mrs. Bing"*

THE ONE ABOUT THE BEAUTY OF MOTHERHOOD

JOEY: How could you let this happen?

ROSS: I don't know. Well, it's not like she's a regular mom. She's, she's sexy, she's—

JOEY: You don't think my mom's sexy?

ROSS: Well, not in the same way—

JOEY: Hey, I'll have you know that Gloria Tribbiani was a handsome woman in her day all right. You think it's easy giving birth to seven children?

ROSS: Okay, I think we're getting into a weird area here.

> —*A Freudian nightmare of a conversation in "The One with Mrs. Bing"*

THE ONE ABOUT FAMILY AFFAIRS

JOEY: . . . You broke the code.
ROSS: What code?
JOEY: You don't kiss your friend's mom. Sisters are okay, maybe a hot-lookin' aunt, but not a mom, never a mom!

> —*Some solid rules in "The One with Mrs. Bing"*

THE ONE ABOUT LITERARY ENDEAVOR

RACHEL: I thought I'd give it a shot. I'm still on the first chapter. Do you think his "love stick can be liberated from its denim prison"?
Monica: (READING A LITTLE) Yeah! I'd say so. (THEN POINTING) And, uh, there's no "j" in "engorged."

> —*A writer seeks to perfect her craft in "The One with Mrs. Bing"*

THE ONE ABOUT STANDING BY YOUR MAN

PHOEBE: (SUNG) You don't have to be awake to be my man/ As long as you have brain waves I'll be there to hold your hand.

> —*A song that Phoebe sings for her ideal, if comatose, love interest in "The One with Mrs. Bing"*

THE ONE ABOUT GREEK TRAGEDY

CHANDLER: . . . Hey, you kissed my mom!
ROSS: (TO THE PATRONS) We're rehearsing a Greek play.

> —*The guilty mother-kisser Ross tries to cover up what he's done to everyone at Central Perk in "The One with Mrs. Bing"*

THE ONE ABOUT COURTING YOUR FRIEND'S MOTHER

CHANDLER: Look, just because you played tonsil tennis with my mom doesn't mean you know her.
—*A son's point of view in "The One with Mrs. Bing"*

THE ONE ABOUT MAKING OUT WITH YOUR SON'S PAL

CHANDLER: (IN A BLURT) You kissed my best Ross! Or something to that effect.
—*A moment of confrontation in "The One with Mrs. Bing"*

THE ONE ABOUT GAY LITERATURE

ROSS: (RE: BOOKSHELVES) Wow, you guys sure have a lot of books about being a lesbian.
SUSAN: (DEADPAN) Well, you know, you have to take a course. Otherwise, they don't let you do it.
—*A secret revealed in "The One Where Underdog Gets Away"*

THE ONE ABOUT BABIES AND BAGELS

ROSS: Hey, hey, you're my baby/ And I can't wait to meet you/ When you get out I'll buy you a bagel/ And then we'll go to the zoo! /Hey, hey, I'm your daddy/ I'm the one without any breasts.
—*Some moving lyrics that Ross sings to the tune of The Monkees theme to his unborn son in "The One Where Underdog Gets Away"*

THE ONE ABOUT THE HOLIDAY SPIRIT

CHANDLER: (LIFTING GLASS) I'd like to propose a toast. Little toast here. I know this isn't the Thanksgiving any of you planned. But for me, this has been really great, mostly because it didn't involve divorce or projectile vomiting.

—*Special, warm seasonal thoughts from the show's resident cynic in "The One Where Underdog Gets Away"*

THE ONE ABOUT THE PREPARED PAPA

JOEY: Ross, did you really read all these baby books?
ROSS: Yep. You could plunk me down in the middle of any woman's uterus, no compass, and I could find my way out of there (SNAPS FINGERS) like that.

—*A confident father-to-be's declaration in "The One with the Dozen Lasagnas"*

THE ONE ABOUT THE DEMANDS OF FAMILY

MONICA: (INTO THE PHONE) Aunt Syl . . . I did this as a favor. I'm not a caterer. What do you want me to do with a dozen lasagnas? . . . Nice talk, Aunt Syl. You kill Uncle Freddie with that mouth?

—*A tense discussion in "The One with the Dozen Lasagnas"*

THE ONE ABOUT GENDER-BENDING FRIENDS

ROSS: Hey. When did you and Susan meet Huey Lewis?
CAROL: Uh, that's our friend Tanya.

—*While looking at some photos, Ross makes an embarrassing mistake in "The One with the Dozen Lasagnas"*

THE ONE ABOUT ROMANTIC TIMING

JOEY: Yes, now is when you swoop. You gotta make sure that when Paolo walks outta there, the first guy Rachel sees is *you*. She's gotta know that you're everything he's not. You're, like, the Anti-Paolo.

CHANDLER: My Catholic friend is right. She's distraught, you're there for her, you pick up the pieces, and then you usher in the Age of Ross.

　　—Ross gets some friendly advice in "The One with the Dozen Lasagnas"

THE ONE ABOUT SEEING GAY

MONICA: . . . You—you just . . . have a quality.

EVERYONE: Yeah. A quality. That's it.

CHANDLER: Oh, a "quality." Good, because I was worried you guys were going to be vague about this.

　　—Chandler tries to understand why some people are under the impression he's not straight in "The One Where Nana Dies Twice"

TERMS OF ENDEARMENT

WENUS (acronym)—Chandler's big business term, which, of course, stands for Weekly Estimated Net Usage System. *Note*: There are some authorities who claim the "S" actually stands for Statistics.

ANUS (acronym)—another of Chandler's business terms, this one standing for Annual Net Usage System. *Note:* There are some authorities who claim the "S" actually stands for Statistics.

THE ONE ABOUT SEEING GAY (PART TWO)

PHOEBE: Yeah. You have homosexual hair.

　　—Phoebe puts her finger on that quality in "The One Where Nana Dies Twice"

THE ONE ABOUT THE DEATH-DEFYING GRANDMOTHER

ROSS: You know how, uh, the nurse said that Nana has passed? Well, she's . . . not quite.

JUDY: What?

ROSS: She's not passed. She's present. She's back.

—*Ross tries to explain to his mother that Nana has returned from the dead in "The One Where Nana Dies Twice"*

THE ONE ABOUT MOTHERHOOD

JUDY: Do you know what it's like to grow up with someone who is critical of every single thing you do?

MONICA: I . . . can imagine.

JUDY: I'm telling you, it's a wonder your mother turned out to be the positive, life-affirming person she is.

—*A mother-daughter moment in "The One Where Nana Dies Twice"*

THE ONE ABOUT HIGH PRAISE

CHANDLER: (ENRAPTURED) She's amazing. She makes women that I dream about look like short, fat, bald men.

—*A lusty compliment in "The One with the Butt"*

THE ONE ABOUT MONOGAMY

CHANDLER: So, explain something to me here. What kind of relationship do you imagine us having if you already have a husband and a boyfriend?

AURORA: I suppose mainly sexual.

—*Sexy, frank talk from Chandler's dream woman in "The One with the Butt"*

THE ONE ABOUT AN ACTOR'S LIFE

PHOEBE: . . . I really believe big things are going to happen for you. I do. And you've just got to keep thinking about the day some kid's gonna run up and tell his friends: "I got the part! I got the part! I'm gonna be Joey Tribbiani's ass."

—Encouraging words for a frustrated thespian in "The One with the Butt"

THE ONE ABOUT THE WEIRDEST PLACE YOU'VE HAD SEX

ROSS: Disneyland. 1989. "It's a Small World After All."
EVERYONE: Get out! No way!
ROSS: The ride broke down. So, Carol and I went behind a couple of mechanical Dutch children . . . Then they fixed the ride, and we were asked never to return to the Magic Kingdom.

—True confessions from the gang in "The One with the Blackout"

THE ONE ABOUT DAIRY

PHOEBE: New York City has no power/ And the milk is getting sour/ But to me it is not scary/ 'cause I stay away from dairy.

—Some graceful lyrics from the veggie singer-songwriter in "The One with the Blackout"

THE ONE ABOUT COMPARATIVE SEX APPEAL

RACHEL: God, the first time he smiled at me . . . those three seconds were more exciting than three weeks in Bermuda with Barry.

—The young lover sizes up her new guy and her old orthodontist in "The One with the Blackout"

THE ONE ABOUT TECHNICALITIES

PAOLO: Ah. You have . . . the sex?

ROSS: No. No no. Technically, the sex is not being had.
  —*Ross confesses an annoying detail of his relationship with Rachel in "The One with the Blackout"*

THE ONE ABOUT PERSONAL BANKING

CHANDLER: (INTO CAMERA) Hi. Um, I'm account number 714357457. And, uh, I don't know if you got any of that, but I would really like a copy of the tape.
  —*An understandable request after Chandler gets kissed by Jill Goodacre in "The One with the Blackout"*

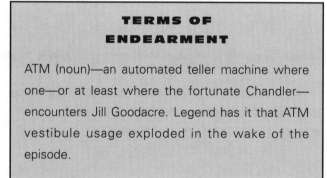

TERMS OF ENDEARMENT

ATM (noun)—an automated teller machine where one—or at least where the fortunate Chandler— encounters Jill Goodacre. Legend has it that ATM vestibule usage exploded in the wake of the episode.

THE ONE ABOUT THE GREAT SNACK DEBATE

CHANDLER: I can't believe you would actually say that. I would *much* rather be Mr. Peanut than Mr. Salty.

JOEY: No way. Mr. Salty is a sailor. He's gotta be, like, the toughest snack there is.

ROSS: I don't know. You don't want to mess with Corn Nuts. They're *craaazy*.

  —A pressing issue is confronted in "The One with the Evil Orthodontist"

THE ONE ABOUT SEX IN THE DENTIST'S CHAIR

RACHEL: I'm not crazy, right? I mean, it was *never* like that . . .

BARRY: Noooo, it wasn't.

RACHEL: And it's so nice having the little sink here.

  —Postcoital chatter in "The One with the Evil Orthodontist"

THE ONE ABOUT SECOND CHANCES

BARRY: (TO MINDY) I swear to you, whatever I was doing, I was always thinking of you.

RACHEL: Oh, please. During that second time, you couldn't have picked her out of a lineup!

MINDY: (ASIDE TO RACHEL) You did it twice.

RACHEL: Well, the first time didn't really count. You know Barry.

  —The horny Barry's shortcomings are alluded to in "The One with the Evil Orthodontist"

THE ONE ABOUT LOVE, MARRIAGE, AND ORTHODONTURE

MINDY: Yeah . . . I'm pretty sure I'm still going to marry him.

RACHEL: What are you talking about? Mindy, the guy's the devil! He's Satan in a smock!

MINDY: Look, I know he's not perfect. But the truth is . . . at the end of the day, I still really want to be Mrs. Dr. Barry Farber, DDS.

> —*Rachel's onetime maid of honor explains her intentions in "The One with the Evil Orthodontist"*

THE ONE ABOUT ANSWERING-MACHINE ETIQUETTE

PHOEBE: If you want, call her machine. If she has a lot of beeps, it probably means she hasn't picked up her messages yet.

CHANDLER: You don't think that seems a little . . .

ROSS: Desperate? Needy? Pathetic?

CHANDLER: You obviously saw my personal ad.

> —*The king of self-deprecation reigns in "The One with the Evil Orthodontist"*

THE ONE ABOUT ANSWERING-MACHINE ETIQUETTE (PART TWO)

CHANDLER: She obviously got my message. And is choosing not to call me. Now I'm needy and *snubbed*. God, I miss just being needy.

> —*In "The One with the Evil Orthodontist"*

THE ONE ABOUT ABSTINENCE

ROSS: Whoa. What—what happened to "forget relationships," "I'm done with men," the whole "penis embargo"?

> —*A subtle plea for Rachel to return to the monastic life in "The One Where the Monkey Gets Away"*

THE ONE ABOUT THE DIFFERENCE BETWEEN HUGH AND LOU GRANT

JOEY: Hey, I don't need violence to enjoy a movie. So long as there's a little nudity.

MONICA: There was nudity.

JOEY: I mean female nudity. I don't need to see Lou Grant frolicking—

MONICA/PHOEBE/CHANDLER: Hugh! Hugh Grant!

> —*An understandable mistake in "The One Where the Monkey Gets Away"*

THE ONE ABOUT ANTIQUE PICKUP TECHNIQUES

ROSS: I figured after work, I'd pick up a bottle of wine, go over there, and try to . . . woo her.

CHANDLER: Hey, you know what you should do? Take her back to the 1890s when that phrase was last used.

> —*A smart-ass dating suggestion in "The One Where the Monkey Gets Away"*

THE ONE ABOUT MONKEY VACATION HABITS

JOEY: All right. You're a monkey. You're loose in the city. Where do you go?

CHANDLER: Okay, it's his first time out, so he's probably going to want to do some of the touristy things. I'll go to *Cats*, you go to the Russian Tea Room.

> —*The search begins in "The One Where the Monkey Gets Away"*

THE ONE ABOUT THE EVOLUTION OF THE SPECIES

ADMISSIONS WOMAN: Sir, this hospital is for people.

ROSS: Lady, he *is* people! He has a name! He watches *Jeopardy!* He touches himself when nobody's looking!

> —*A semi-Darwinian argument at the hospital in "The One with Two Parts, Part Two"*

THE ONE ABOUT BOARDING SCHOOL

JOEY: I loved high school. You know, it was just, like, four years of parties and dating and sex . . .

CHANDLER: Yeah, well, I went to boarding school with four hundred boys. Any sex I had would have involved a major lifestyle choice.

> —*Chandler recalls his sexless school days in "The One Where the Monkey Gets Away"*

THE ONE ABOUT FATHERHOOD AND FOOTBALL

ROSS: I had a dream last night where I was playing football with my kid.

CHANDLER: Oh, yeah? That's nice.

ROSS: No. No. (ILLUSTRATING) *With* him. I'm on this field, and they hike me the baby. And I know I've got to do something, 'cause the Tampa Bay defense is coming right at me.

> —*Winning fatherly chatter in "The One with Two Parts, Part Two"*

THE ONE ABOUT THE HIGHLY ATTRACTIVE MEDICAL FIELD

RACHEL: (TO DR. ROSEN) Aren't you a little cute to be a doctor?

DR. ROSEN: Excuse me?

RACHEL: (MORTIFIED) Oh, I meant, God, "young." *Young* to be a doctor. Good, Rach.

> —*Doctor-enthusiast Rachel trips on her tongue in "The One with Two Parts, Part Two"*

THE ONE ABOUT FINE WINE

DR. ROSEN: Here. We brought wine.

DR. MITCHELL: And look: It's from the cellars of Ernest and Tova Borgnine. How could we resist?

> —*Those familiar ER doctors share their good spirits in "The One with Two Parts, Part Two"*

THE ONE ABOUT THE HUMMUS

DR. ROSEN: (UNCOMFORTABLE) This hummus is great.
DR. MITCHELL: (AFTER A MOMENT) God bless the chick-pea.
　　—*Slightly awkward food chatter in "The One with Two Parts, Part Two"*

THE ONE ABOUT ROLE REVERSAL

RACHEL: I shoplift.
MONICA: Hey. That was years ago. And you had no idea that lipstick was in your purse. Did I mention that I think I'm much cuter than I am?
RACHEL: By the way, in high school, I was a cow.
MONICA: I used to wet my bed.
RACHEL: I use my breasts to get people's attention.
MONICA: Hey, we both do that.

　　—*The roommates switch names and engage in a little cat scratch fever in "The One with Two Parts, Part Two"*

ON THE PERILS OF SCRABBLE

PHOEBE: How's he doing?
ROSS: The doctor got the "K" out. He also found an "M" and an "O."
CHANDLER: We think he was trying to spell "MONKEY."
　　—*Marcel has a red-letter day in "The One with Two Parts, Part Two"*

THE ONE ABOUT CAREERS IN JOURNALISM

MONICA: (READING ENVELOPE) Do you really want a job with *Popular Mechanics*?
CHANDLER: Well, if you're gonna work for mechanics, those are the ones to work for.
　　—*Monica gets her hands dirty in "The One with All the Poker"*

THE ONE ABOUT LONGING

CHANDLER: Could you want her more?

ROSS: (ALL INNOCENCE) Who?

CHANDLER: Dee, the sarcastic sister from *What's Happening!!*
   —*Chandler prods Ross about his love for Rachel in "The One with All the Poker"*

THE ONE ABOUT GAMBLING

PHOEBE: (TO JOEY) I see. So, then, you were lying.

JOEY: About what?

PHOEBE: About how good your cards were.

JOEY: I was bluffing.

PHOEBE: (CLARENCE DARROW) Aha. And what is "bluffing"? Is it not another word for . . . "*lying*"!?
   —*A little gambling debate in "The One with All the Poker"*

THE ONE ABOUT GETTING YOUR YA-YAS

RACHEL: So, basically, you get your ya-yas by taking money from your friends.

ROSS: Yeah.

CHANDLER: (ASIDE) I get my ya-yas from Ikea. You have to put them together yourself, but they cost a little less.
   —*A shopping tip in "The One with All the Poker"*

THE ONE ABOUT SUGARLESS GUM

RACHEL: Guys! Guess what, guess what, guess what, guess what?

CHANDLER: Uh, okay. The fifth dentist caved? Now they're *all* recommending Trident?
   —*An off-the-cuff guess in "The One with All the Poker"*

THE ONE ABOUT THE BEAUTY
OF SISTERHOOD

CHANDLER: (INDICATING PHOEBE) All right. Now look at her. Tell me she doesn't look *exactly* like her sister.

JOEY: I'm saying, I see a difference.

CHANDLER: They're twins!

JOEY: I don't care. Phoebe's Phoebe. Ursula's . . . hot.

CHANDLER: You know that thing when you and I talk to each other about things?

JOEY: Yeah.

CHANDLER: Let's not do that anymore.

> *—A friendly chat in "The One with Two Parts, Part One"*

THE ONE ABOUT THE BEAUTY OF SISTERHOOD
(PART TWO)

JOEY: You think it would be okay if I asked out your sister?

PHOEBE: (THROWN) Why—why would you want to do that? Why?

JOEY: So that if we went out on a date, she'd be there?

PHOEBE: Well . . . I mean I'm not my sister's, you know, whatever. And, uhm, I mean, it's true we were one egg once, but, uhm, we've grown apart.

> *—Tense but friendly negotiations in "The One with Two Parts, Part Two"*

THE ONE ABOUT BLIND GUESSING

JOEY: (TO PHOEBE) Hey, Pheebs, guess who we saw today?

PHOEBE: Ooo, ooo, fun. Liam Neeson! Morley Safer! The woman who cuts my hair!

MONICA: Okay, look, this could be a really long game.

> *—Some dada dialogue in "The One with Two Parts, Part One"*

THE ONE ABOUT SIBLING RIVALRY

PHOEBE: It's mostly dumb sister stuff. You know, I mean like everyone always thought of her as "the pretty one." You know, and oh oh, she was the first to start walking. Even though I did it, later the same day, but to my parents by then it was like, "Right, what else is new?"

> —*Phoebe shares her pain regarding her sister Ursula in "The One with Two Parts, Part One"*

THE ONE ABOUT MISTAKEN IDENTITY

FRAN: What's she doing here?

JAMIE: This could be God's way of telling us "eat at home."

> —*The women of* Mad About You *react to seeing who they think is Ursula at Central Perk in "The One with Two Parts, Part One"*

THE ONE ABOUT BIRTHDAY GIFTS

RACHEL: So, Pheebs. What do you want for your birthday?

PHOEBE: Well . . . what I really want is for my mom to be alive to enjoy it with me.

RACHEL: Okaay . . . Let me put it this way: Anything from Crabtree & Evelyn?

PHOEBE: Bath salts would be nice.

> —*Rachel negotiates her friend down in "The One with Two Parts, Part One"*

THE ONE ABOUT THE JOY OF CHILDBIRTH

CAROL: What that woman . . . did. I'm not doing that. (INDICATING HER BELLY) It's just gonna have to stay in, that's all. Everything'll be the same, it'll just stay in.

ROSS: Carol. Honey. Shh. Everything's gonna be alright.

CAROL: Oh, what do you know?! No one's going up to you saying, "Hi. Is that your nostril? Mind if we push this pot roast through it?!"

—Ross' wife expressing some doubts about her impending mother-hood in "The One with Two Parts, Part One"

THE ONE ABOUT THE PAIN OF BREAKING UP

JANICE: (TO CHANDLER) By the way, Chandler . . . I cut you out of all my pictures. So, if you want, I have a bag with just your heads.

CHANDLER: That's okay.

JANICE: Oh, are you sure? 'Cause you could make little puppets and you could use them in your theater of *cruelty*.

—A tortured moment in "The One with the Candy Hearts"

THE ONE ABOUT GREAT PICKUP LINES

JOEY: She said she wants to slather my body with stuff and lick it off me. I'm not even sure what "slathering" is, but I definitely wanna be a part of it.

—A turned-on Joey wanting to extend his vocabulary in "The One with the Candy Hearts"

THE ONE ABOUT THE LOST ART OF MAKING CONVERSATION

ROSS: I'm just saying if dogs *do* experience jetlag, then, because of this whole "seven dog years to one human year" thing, when a dog flies from New York to Los Angeles, he doesn't just lose three hours. He loses, like, a week and a half.

—An informative observation in "The One with the Candy Hearts"

THE ONE ABOUT LOOKING FOR THE RIGHT WOMAN

CAROL: You'll find someone. I know you will. The right woman is just waiting for you.

ROSS: That's easy for *you* to say. You found one already.

—A Valentine's Day exchange in "The One with the Candy Hearts"

THE ONE ABOUT INSPIRATIONAL ORATORS IN OUR TIME

CHANDLER: (TO ALL BUT RACHEL) Hey, you guys in the living room all know what you want to do. You know, you have goals. You have dreams. I don't have a dream.

ROSS: Ah, the lesser known "I Don't Have a Dream" speech.

—A kingly comment in "The One with the Stoned Guy"

THE ONE ABOUT OFFICE POLITICS

CHANDLER: Ms. Tedlock. You're looking lovely today. And may I say, that is a *very* flattering sleeve length on you.

—Chandler kisses ass at work in "The One with the Stoned Guy"

THE ONE ABOUT RED MEAT

ROSS: Hey, guys. Does anybody know a good date place in the neighborhood?

JOEY: How 'bout Tony's. If you can finish a thirty-two-ounce steak, it's free.

ROSS: Okay. Hey, does anyone know a good place if you're not dating a puma?

—A dating and dining debate in "The One with the Stoned Guy"

THE ONE ABOUT THE HIGH LIFE

RACHEL: What's up?

PHOEBE: (WHISPERED) In the cab on the way over, Steve blazed up a doobie.

RACHEL: What?

PHOEBE: Smoked a joint? Lit a bone? Weed? Hemp? Ganja?

—A rare druggy moment in "The One with the Stoned Guy"

THE ONE ABOUT AMBITIOUS SMUT

ROSS: I was the James Michener of dirty talk. It was the most elaborate filth you have *ever* heard. I mean, there were different characters, plot lines, themes, a motif. At one point there were villagers . . .

—A breakthrough moment in dirty talk in "The One with the Stoned Guy"

THE ONE ABOUT A ROCK AND A HARD PLACE

CHANDLER: You know, I don't know why you're so embarrassed. They were very nice boobies.

RACHEL: (TO CHANDLER) "Nice"? They were "nice"? I mean, that's it? I mean, mittens are "nice."

CHANDLER: (ILLUSTRATING) Okay. Rock. Hard place. Me.

—Chandler digs himself into a hole in "The One with the Boobies"

THE ONE ABOUT HUMOR AS A DEFENSE

ROGER: (LAUGHING) You are so funny. (TO PHOEBE) He's really funny.

CHANDLER: (MR. MODESTY) Well . . .

ROGER: Of course, I wouldn't want to be there (AIR QUOTES) "when the laughter stops."

—Phoebe's psychologist boy toy offers some instant shrinkage in "The One with the Boobies"

THE ONE ABOUT BEING TORN BETWEEN TWO LOVERS

JOEY SR.: Joe, your dad's in love big time. And the worst part is, it's with *two* different women.

JOEY: Oh, man. Please tell me one of 'em's Ma.

—Joey and his dad get to the heart of the issue in "The One with the Boobies"

THE ONE ABOUT TURNABOUT BEING FAIR PLAY

ROSS: Since you saw her boobies, I think you're going to have to show her your pee-pee.

CHANDLER: You know, I don't see that happening.

RACHEL: Come on. He's right. Tit for tat.

CHANDLER: Well, I am not showing you my tat.

—A search for justice in "The One with the Boobies"

THE ONE ABOUT ROLE REVERSAL

JOEY: That's right, mister. I don't care how old you are, as long as you're under my roof, you're gonna live by my rules. And that means no sleeping with your girlfriend.

—Joey lays down the law to his father in "The One with the Boobies"

THE ONE ABOUT FRIENDLY DYSFUNCTION

ROGER: Actually, it's quite, you know, typical behavior when you have this kind of dysfunctional group dynamic. You know, this sort of codependent, emotionally stunted, sitting in your stupid coffeehouse, with your stupid big cups—which, I'm sorry, might as well have *nipples* on them. And you're all like: (WHINY VOICE) "I need love! I need love! Define me! Define me! Love me! I need love! . . ."

—The bitter but professional reading of the friends' group dynamics in "The One with the Boobies"

THE ONE ABOUT THE BENEFITS OF ADULTERY

GLORIA: Remember how your father used to be? Always yelling? Always yelling, nothing made him happy? Not that woodshop. Not those stupid little ships in the bottle. Now he's happy. I mean, it's nice. He has a hobby.
— *Joey's mom explains her support for her husband's cheating in "The One with the Boobies"*

THE ONE ABOUT CONTEMPORARY AMERICAN FAMILY LIFE

JOEY: Yeah. He's gonna keep cheating on my ma, like she wanted. My ma's gonna keep pretending she doesn't know, even though she does. And my little sister Tina can't see her husband anymore 'cause he got a restraining order—which has nothing to do with anything, except I found out today.
RACHEL: Wow.
CHANDLER: Things sure have changed here on Walton's Mountain.
— *A warm family moment in "The One with the Boobies"*

THE ONE ABOUT "LIKING" PROBLEMS

ROGER: What's wrong, sweetie?
PHOEBE: Nothing. Nothing. I'm fine. It's just, um . . . it's my friends. They have a "liking" problem with you. In that, um, they don't.
— *Phoebe diagnoses her friends' problems with her shrink boyfriend in "The One with the Boobies"*

THE ONE ABOUT CONTEMPORARY AMERICAN FAMILY LIFE (PART TWO)

JOEY: It's just, you know, they're parents. After a certain point, you gotta let go. Even if you know better, you gotta let them make their own mistakes.
RACHEL: And just think, in a couple of years, we get to turn into them.
CHANDLER: If I turn into my parents, I'll either be an alcoholic blond chasing twenty-year-old boys, or . . . I'll wind up like my mom.
— *More family fun in "The One with the Boobies"*

THE ONE ABOUT GETTING THE MONKEY

ROSS: My friend, Bethel, rescued him from some lab.

PHOEBE: That's so cruel. Why would a parent name their child Bethel?

—Phoebe's sensitive comment on human cruelty in "The One with the Monkey"

THE ONE ABOUT ROOMMATES

MONICA: Why don't you just get a roommate?

ROSS: I dunno, I think you reach a certain age and having a roommate is kinda path—(OFF EVERYONE'S LOOKS) sorry, that's pathetic, which is Sanskrit for "really cool way to live."

—Ross tries to save himself in "The One with the Monkey"

THE ONE ABOUT PHOEBE'S MUSE

PHOEBE: I'm doing all new material tonight. I have twelve new songs about my mother's suicide and one about a snowman.

CHANDLER: Uh, you might want to open with the snowman.

—A useful sequencing tip in "The One with the Monkey"

THE ONE ABOUT COMPARATIVE COURTING

RACHEL: Pheebs, I can't believe he hasn't kissed you yet. God, by my sixth date with Paolo, he'd already named both my breasts. Did I share too much?

ROSS: Just a smidge.

—More than Ross cared to know in "The One with the Monkey"

THE ONE ABOUT FIGHTING AND FECES

ROSS: Look, I didn't want to leave him alone. We had our first fight this morning. I think it has to do with my working late. I said some things I didn't mean. He threw some feces.

—An emotional moment in "The One with the Monkey"

THE ONE ABOUT THE LIMITS OF SCIENCE

MAX: Tell her, David. (AS DAVID) "No, I don't want to go to Minsk and work with Lifson and Yamaguchi and Flench. No—no no no! I want to stay here and make out with my girlfriend!"

—An angry scientific disagreement among colleagues in "The One with the Monkey"

THE ONE ABOUT UNUSUAL SEASONAL GREETINGS

SANDY: You know, when I saw you at the store last week, it was probably the first time I ever mentally undressed an elf.

—A brief love interest of Joey's makes a holiday confession in "The One with the Birth"

THE ONE ABOUT OLD-FASHIONED FATHERHOOD

MONICA: Joey, what are you going to do when you have a baby?

JOEY: I'm gonna be in the waiting room, handing out cigars.

CHANDLER: Yes. Joey's made arrangements to have his baby in a movie from the fifties.

—A generational point in "The One with the Birth"

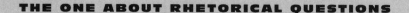

THE ONE ABOUT RHETORICAL QUESTIONS

MONICA: Is there something fundamentally *unmarryable* about me?
CHANDLER: (SCRAMBLING) Uh . . .
MONICA: Well??
CHANDLER: (PULLING AN IMAGINARY RIPCORD) Dear God, this parachute is a knapsack.

> —*A no-win situation in "The One with the Birth"*

THE ONE ABOUT THE NAME GAME

ROSS: I don't have a son named Jordie. We all agreed my son's name is *Jamie*.
CAROL: (END OF CONTRACTION) Aaaaah . . . Well, "Jamie" was the name of Susan's first girlfriend, so we went back to Jordie.
ROSS: Whoa. What do you mean *back* to Jordie? We never landed on "Jordie." We just passed by it during the whole Jesse/Cody/Dylan fiasco.

> —*The interested parties discuss the baby's name in "The One with the Birth"*

THE ONE ABOUT CONTEMPORARY AMERICAN FAMILY LIFE (PART THREE)

ROSS: And you know what the funny thing is, when this day is over, you get to go home with the baby—okay. Where does that leave me?
SUSAN: *You* get to be the baby's father. Everyone knows who you are. Who am I? There's Father's Day and Mother's Day. There's no . . . Lesbian Lover's Day!
ROSS: *Every* day is Lesbian Lover's Day!

> —*The two people who love Carol most hash it out in "The One with the Birth"*

THE ONE ABOUT CONTEMPORARY AMERICAN FAMILY LIFE (PART FOUR)

NURSE: So, anybody who's not an ex-husband or a lesbian life partner, out you go.

EVERYONE: (FILING OUT) Good luck. Hang in there. You're having a baby!

CHANDLER: Let me ask you, do you have to be *Carol's* lesbian life partner?

—*Ross examines a fine point in "The One with the Birth"*

THE ONE ABOUT THE JOY OF CHILDBIRTH (PART TWO)

CAROL: What does he look like?

ROSS: (STUDYING HIM) Kind of like my Uncle Ed covered in Jell-O.

—*Ross notices a family resemblance in "The One with the Birth"*

THE ONE ABOUT GENETICS

PHOEBE: Susan, he looks just like you!

SUSAN: (BEAMING) Thanks.

RACHEL: Oh God I can't believe one of us actually *has* one of these!

CHANDLER: I know. I still *am* one of these.

—*The gang greets new arrival Ben in "The One with the Birth"*

THE ONE ABOUT GUM

MONICA: (MOVED) Hi, Ben. Hi. I'm your Aunt Monica. I—I will always have gum.

—*A new aunt's moving pledge in "The One with the Birth"*

THE ONE ABOUT ANIMAL HUSBANDRY

MONICA: Ross, you've really got to do something about this humping.

ROSS: What? It's just a phase.

CHANDLER: That's what we said about Joey.

ROSS: Would you all relax? It's not that big a deal.

RACHEL: Marcel! Stop it, Marcel! Bad monkey!

ROSS: What?

RACHEL: Let's just say my Curious George doll is no longer curious.

—The end of Marcel's innocence in "The One with the Fake Monica"

THE ONE ABOUT HAVING THE BEST OF BOTH WORLDS

MONICA: She's got everything I want. And she *doesn't* have my mother!

—Monica's jealous thought about her secret sharer in "The One with the Fake Monica"

THE ONE ABOUT THE HUMPING THING

ROSS: I just got back from the vet.

CHANDLER: She's not going to make you wear one of those big, plastic cones, is she?

ROSS: She says Marcel's humping thing's not a phase. Apparently, he's reached sexual maturity.

JOEY: (TO CHANDLER) Hey, he beat ya.

—A difficult diagnosis in "The One with the Fake Monica"

THE ONE ABOUT THE HUMPING THING (PART TWO)

ROSS: I mean, one day he was this little thing. And then, before you know it, he's this little thing I can't get off my leg.

—A comment on how fast they grow up in "The One with the Fake Monica"

THE ONE ABOUT PARTING ADVICE

CHANDLER: (TO MARCEL) Okay, bye, champ. Now, I know there's going to be a lot of babes in San Diego, but remember . . . there's also a lot to learn.

> —*A family friend gives the monkey some solid advice before he goes off to the zoo in "The One with the Fake Monica"*

THE ONE ABOUT THE SEX DREAM

ROSS: Why—why—why would you dream that?

CHANDLER: More importantly: Was I any good?

RACHEL: (WITH AN EMBARRASSED SMILE) You were pretty damn "any good."

CHANDLER: Interesting. 'Cause in *my* dreams, I'm surprisingly inadequate.

> —*Rachel's dream tryst with Chandler gets everyone riled up in "The One with the Ick Factor"*

THE ONE ABOUT THE SEX DREAM (PART TWO)

ROSS: I can't believe you two had sex in her dream.

CHANDLER: I'm sorry, man. It was a onetime thing. I was very drunk, it was somebody else's subconscious.

> —*Further ruminations on a sexual nonact in "The One with the Ick Factor"*

THE ONE ABOUT ROBBING THE CRADLE

MONICA: What we did was wrong! Oh God. I just had sex with someone who wasn't alive during the bicentennial!

> —*An older woman's horrible realization in "The One with the Ick Factor"*

THE ONE ABOUT COMMON MISCONCEPTIONS

ETHAN: I'm telling you. Up until I was, like, nine, I thought that "gun-point" was an actual place where crimes happened.

MONICA: How is that possible?

ETHAN: Well, think about it. It was always in the news: "A man is being held up at gunpoint." "Tourists are being terrorized at gunpoint." And I just kept thinking: Why do people continue to go there?

> *—Monica's young lover opens up to her in "The One with the Ick Factor"*

THE ONE ABOUT ROBBING THE CRADLE (PART TWO)

MONICA: You shouldn't even be here! It's—it's a school night! Oh God, I'm like those women you see with shiny guys named Chad. I'm Joan Collins.

ETHAN: Who?

> *—The generation gap emerges in "The One with the Ick Factor"*

THE ONE ABOUT ROBBING THE CRADLE (PART THREE)

ROSS: And you're not seeing him anymore?

MONICA: (EVASIVE) No. You know, sometimes things just . . . don't work out.

CHANDLER: And this has nothing to do with the fact that he needs a note to get out of gym?

> *—The friends quiz Monica about breaking up with young Ethan in "The One with the Ick Factor"*

THE ONE ABOUT FOLLOWING YOUR BLISS
(PART TWO)

PHOEBE: Wow! You're gonna make money hand over fist.

—*The group's impressed with Joey's job contributing intimately to a fertility project in "The One Where Rachel Finds Out"*

THE ONE ABOUT PRIMITIVE MAN

CHANDLER: (CAVEMAN VOICE) Men are here.

JOEY: (CAVEMAN VOICE) We make fire. Cook meat.

CHANDLER: (CAVEMAN VOICE) Then put out fire by peeing. No get invited back.

—*The guys get in touch with their primal manliness in "The One Where Rachel Finds Out"*

THE ONE ABOUT THE DOWNSIDE OF
FOLLOWING YOUR OWN BLISS

JOEY: The tough thing is, she really wants to have sex with me.

CHANDLER: That crazy bitch.

JOEY: Yeah, well, I still got a week left to go on the program. And according to the rules, if I want to get the money, I'm not allowed to conduct any . . . personal "experiments," if you know what I mean.

MONICA: Joey, we always know what you mean.

—*A temporarily monastic Joey grapples with how to deal with a lusty girlfriend in "The One Where Rachel Finds Out"*

THE ONE ABOUT PALEONTOLOGY

MONICA: You're going to *China*??

ROSS: (NOT WANTING TO GET INTO IT) It's for the museum. Someone found a bone. We want the bone. They don't want us to have the bone. I'm going to try to persuade them to give us the bo— It's a whole big bone thing.

—*Ross gets technical about his work in "The One Where Rachel Finds Out"*

THE ONE ABOUT CHINESE CUISINE

CHANDLER: Forget about her!

JOEY: He's right, man. Please. Move on. Go to China. Eat Chinese food.

CHANDLER: Of course, there they just call it "food."

—The guys offer Ross some advice in "The One Where Rachel Finds Out"

THE ONE ABOUT THE INNER CHILD

MELANIE: (SNUGGLING UP TO JOEY) There is a little child inside this man.

CHANDLER: Yes, the doctors say if they remove it, he'll die.

—A New Agey warning in "The One Where Rachel Finds Out"

THE ONE ABOUT SPILLING THE BEANS
(PART TWO)

RACHEL: This is unbelievable. This is unbelievable.

PHOEBE: I know. This is really, really huge.

CHANDLER: No it's not. It's small. It's tiny. It's petite. It's wee.

PHOEBE: Nuh uh. I don't think any of our lives are ever going to be the same ever again.

CHANDLER: Is there a mute button on this woman?

—The moment after Chandler lets on that Ross loves Rachel in "The One Where Rachel Finds Out"

THE ONE ABOUT THE DANGER OF ROMANCE

RACHEL: Ross, you're, like, my best friend. If we broke up, and I lost you . . .

ROSS: What makes you think we're gonna break up?

RACHEL: Well, have you ever been involved with someone where you haven't broken up?

ROSS: (CONSIDERING THIS) No . . . But it only has to happen once.

—A convincing if imaginary point in "The One Where Rachel Finds Out"

THE ONE ABOUT UNUSUAL EXPRESSIONS OF SEXUAL SATISFACTION

MELANIE: Boy, somebody's getting a *big* fruit basket tomorrow.
   —*One of the Three Basketeers' grateful comments in "The One Where Rachel Finds Out"*

THE ONE ABOUT LOUD SEX

CHANDLER: So? How'd it go?
JOEY: (GRINNING) It was amazing. You know how you always think you're great in bed?
CHANDLER: The fact that you even ask that question shows how little you know me.
JOEY: Well, it's like . . . last night, I couldn't do the thing that usually makes me great. So, I had to do all this other stuff. And the response I got . . . man oh man, it was like a ticker-tape parade.
CHANDLER: Yes, I know. As it happens, my room is very, very close to the parade route.
   —*An intimate talk between the apartment mates in "The One Where Rachel Finds Out"*

THE ONE ABOUT GENDER ROLES

MELANIE: I don't know. I guess I just had you pegged as one of those guys who are always "me, me, me." But you, you're a giver. You're like the most generous man I ever met. I mean, you're practically a woman.
   —*More praise for Joey in "The One Where Rachel Finds Out"*

THE ONE ABOUT THE APPROVAL OF FRIENDS

ROSS: I cannot wait for you to meet everybody.
JULIE: Really? You don't think they'll judge and ridicule me?
ROSS: No, no. They will. I—
JULIE: —you just can't wait.
ROSS: Come on, they're gonna love you.
   —*The last words spoken in the cliffhanger ending of the season-closing in "The One Where Rachel Finds Out"*

Friendly Encounters

JENNIFER ANISTON

Formerly spoiled but always lovely, Rachel Karen Green is charming enough to single-handedly make "Princess" a regal compliment again. Before finding modestly gainful employment at Central Perk, Rachel came from the suburbs, where she had apparently been raised like a prized veal.

Her decision to leave her fiancé Barry the Evil Orthodontist at the altar led her to dramatically search out a new life in the big city. Rachel—who we've heard was the queen of her high school—and Monica were childhood friends who'd grown apart for a time. Ross, of course, had a crush on Rachel even back in those old school days. It's not hard to see why.

Part of the charm of Rachel no doubt comes from Jennifer Aniston herself, who grew up around actors—her father John Aniston has been a familiar soap opera actor, while the late Telly Savalas was her godfather. Aniston—also an artist—started acting at Manhattan's Rudolf Steiner School, and went on to attend New York's High School for the Performing Arts, familiar as the Fame school. After graduating in 1987, Aniston did impressive stage work such as *For Dear Life* at the Public Theater. Her TV work, meanwhile, included *Molloy*, *Ferris Bueller*, *The Edge*, and *Muddling Through*. She can also be seen in the 1993 Celtic-themed slasher movie *Leprechaun*. During the summer hiatus, Aniston filmed the upcoming feature film *Dream for an Insomniac* with Ione Skye.

So did seeing your father and Telly Savalas help give you the showbiz bug?

Not really. My father kept me pretty much away from it all. He never wanted me to get into acting. But Telly *did* give me a pink bicycle on my seventh birthday.

What do you remember about the *Friends* auditions?

They wanted me to read for Monica. I said no because I just felt much more of a connection with Rachel.

What did you think when you read the *Friends* pilot script?

The quality was completely obvious. I had never laughed out loud when I read something before. I instantly felt a kinship with the material.

Did you get any good advice when the show starting taking off?

Before everything took off, Jimmy Burrows sat us down at dinner in Las Vegas and told us that the most important thing in the world was to watch out for one another. And we have, and in the process we've all become really close.

How have your old pals reacted?

It may have been a little weird for them because I've been *so* busy. But fortunately I've got a pretty amazing group of friends who understand.

What do you feel makes *Friends* so popular?

First I'd have to say the writing. People—all sorts of people—relate to these characters and the issues dealt with on the show. Whoever you are, you can always identify with *somebody*. I've had a table of grandparents tell me that *Friends* is their favorite show. So obviously we're tapping in at a lot of different levels. And, sad as it is to say, with family being what it is these days, extended groups of friends are *very* important to people.

Was it difficult for you to "play dumb" as Rachel about Ross' crush?

Oh yeah. It was frustrating to be playing this girl that's so oblivious to what's happening. Even *I* wondered, how is Rachel not aware of his feelings?

Why aren't all the friends sleeping together?

If we were living in a different time, maybe we *would* all be sleeping together, you know. I have a similar group of friends, and there have been times when that line has been crossed, and the results were definitely not great.

So how do the women of *Friends* feel about the men of the show?

We have the best group of boys. We love our boys *so* much. I mean, they're the most sensitive, loving, supportive guys.

Sounds like you're all one big mutual-admiration society.

Yeah, no one's jaded. We do get along amazingly. It's kind of sickening, isn't it?

Just a little. Were you bothered when some critics wrote the show off as just a Generation X thing?

We heard that all the time, but no one really knows what it means. I don't think the characters on *Friends* are aimlessly going through life. These characters all have dreams. They have ambitions. They have jobs. They have goals.

Did you do a lot of hands-on research about being a waitress?

I was a waitress for years, so believe me I already knew.

Marta Kauffman has called *Friends* an "overcaffeinated" show. Exactly how much coffee do you folks drink?

Unbelievable. The amount of coffee that I've watched Matthew Perry and David Schwimmer consume is scary.

Any favorite episodes?

"The One with the Blackout," "The One with the East German Laundry Detergent," "The One with the Sonogram at the End." There are so many.

Why was the monkey so unpopular?

I love the monkey. . .when I watch him on TV. But, boy, that friggin' monkey could waste time on the set. It could be cute, cute, cute, then it would go into *Outbreak* mode, and we'd be in trouble.

Since the friends have been compared to The Beatles, which Beatle do you think each of you is most like?

I think we're all Ringo.

COURTENEY COX

The saucy but obsessive Monica Geller is a *nouvelle* beauty who generally serves as a sort of responsible voice of reason for the rest of the *Friend*s gang. When we first met Monica, she was working as the assistant chef at a chic uptown restaurant (apparently it's Iridium on the West Side). Her social life was less than tasty—indeed, she found herself cooking in the kitchen of love with a truly shocking infrequency. An apparent magnet for troubled men, Monica is the friend on *Friends* who seems to have drawn the others into their wonderfully wacky world of endlessly amiable codependency. Ross is her big brother—and apparently the favorite of her parents—while Rachel is a friend from her school days. Overweight growing up, she has obviously blossomed since then.

Cox herself was the most familiar friendly face before the show began. In 1984 she appeared on *As the World Turns*, then made a big, boss splash as Bruce Springsteen's dance partner in the popular "Dancing in the Dark" video. From there, she went on to appear in a number of feature films (*Ace Ventura: Pet Detective, Cocoon: The Return, Down Twisted*), TV movies (*Prize Pulitzer, If It's Tuesday, It Still Must Be Belgium*), and other series (*Misfits of Science*, and the troubled *The Trouble with Larry*). TV viewers everywhere saw Cox play Lauren opposite Michael J. Fox's Alex P. Keaton in *Family Ties*. But nobody ever saw Cox be quite as funny and endearing as she is in the company of *Friends*.

So tell me about your time with the Boss.
We did it at an actual Springsteen concert. We did some close-ups the day before. After all this time, I still can't believe the reaction being in that video got me. Since then I've actually gotten to know him a bit through a mutual friend.

What else had you done before that?
Just two days on a soap, a New York telephone ad, and a commercial for Noxzema. The video was in 1984. It got me into a lot of doors, if only so people could get to ask me about Bruce.

What was the *Family Ties* experience like?
At the time, Michael J. Fox's character getting a new girlfriend was a very big thing. But being on a show that was already a hit was a totally different thing.

When you first heard about *Friends,* did you think the show might be a little contrived?
Yeah, the comedy is absolutely better than the situation. I think the characters make it interesting, not their situations.

You and the other women of *Friends* seem to get along so well. Isn't there any cat-scratch fever going on?
Sorry, but no. It's so rare you get to work with women whom you get along with so well. You know how girls can be. Everybody gets bent sometime, but everyone else gives them their space. I wish I could give you some dirt.

So why hasn't Monica done the deed with Joey or Chandler?
Monica's too smart to sleep with Joey, and Chandler doesn't know how to have a relationship.

How different are you from "our little Harmonica"?
Monica's a little more compulsive than I am, although I'm a pretty compulsive person too. She's also a little more patient than I am. Having all those people hanging around my apartment so much might bug me a little bit.

What's the hardest thing about playing Monica for you?
When I first read the pilot I thought she was more naive than I am. That guy with the come-on line about being impotent—I *never* would have

bought that line. But I believe it actually happened to one of the writers.

Do you feel you and Monica have grown more alike?
Uh huh. We're both developing at the same time.

What do you think makes the show work?
What's so great about this show is that there are six lead characters, and they're *all* interesting. You can't really get bored watching *Friends* as far as I'm concerned. There are so many of us that you get just a little taste of everything. There's no time for you to burn out.

Have you heard from anyone who was shocked by something on the show?
I have friends back in Alabama who were kind of shocked at the Ross situation with his wife leaving him for another woman. I told them, "Are you *nuts*? Your neighbors are probably going through the exact same thing."

Who is most different from the character he or she plays?
Lisa Kudrow, *definitely*.

Do you think *Friends* has a message?
No, but I think we deal with reality. The issues we cover are real. And the language we use is pretty real too. There have been a couple of times when I read the script and thought, "Can we say that on television?" We've said the word "penis." When was the last time you heard *that* on TV?

What do you think is going to happen to the friends long term? Can they hang out together forever without getting pitiful?
Eventually we all might get married, but a show can carry on no matter what happens. Look at Urkel.

LISA KUDROW

Space—the final frontier—is territory that *Friends'* own philosopher queen Phoebe Buffay has covered with extraordinary wit and style. True, you may not have always necessarily understood what this New Agey bohemian babe was talking about, but you loved her nonetheless. Surviving a profoundly screwed-up childhood, "Pheebs"—as she's often affection-

ately called—has found her salvation in her folky music, aromatherapy, and, most of all, in the loving support of her close circle of friends. Of course, she has a twin sister Ursula who can be seen waiting tables badly on *Mad About You*. They are *not* close. There are suggestions that Phoebe was once Monica's room-mate—more recently she's lived with her grandmother. A semi-ditzy Renaissance woman for the nineties, Phoebe is a masseuse, a singer-song-writer with a small but loyal following at Central Perk, and, most of all, an extremely dedicated friend.

Lisa Kudrow, though born in Encino, California, is certainly not your aver-age Valley girl. After graduating with a B.S. in biology from Vassar, she nearly followed in the career path of her father, a well-known headache authority. Instead of pursuing a life of scientific research, Kudrow opted to go into comedy and acting. Early encouragement came from *Saturday Night Live*'s Jon Lovitz, a friend of Kudrow's brother who would later make a memorable *Friends* turn in "The One with the Stoned Guy." After working with The Groundlings—a famed improvisational theater group—Kudrow started turning up all over TV, not only as a semi-regular on *Mad About You*, but also on *Bob, Cheers,* and *Coach*. But it was as Phoebe on *Friends* that Kudrow finally won her big, much-deserved chance to shine on like a crazy diamond.

What do you recollect about your earliest showbiz efforts?
I acted in elementary school—all I remember is that the whole play rhymed. And in junior high, I wrote a sketch spoofing *Family Affair*. I recall that it was a lot of fun bossing all the other kids around, telling them *exactly* how they had to perform the role of Mr. French.

How gradual was the cast bonding on *Friends*?
Not very gradual at all.

Your castmates say that you're worlds away from Phoebe.
I'm actually more jappy, and Jennifer Aniston is a lot more spiritually oriented. Every time we talk, I think she would be a great Phoebe. They wouldn't let me read for Rachel.

Do you find the fact that all the characters haven't coupled off hard to buy?
No. I think they know how it would cloud the relationships. In real life, if you have a group of friends and they start sleeping together, that group won't last very long. I think sometimes men and women just know to stay away from that area.

Since you've made the decision to get married in real life, do you think these single friends on the show will just hang out indefinitely?
I think the good thing is that our audience is just interested in these people *whatever* they do. If someone in the gang gets married, I imagine we'll have tens of millions of people who will want to be watching them.

So what do you suppose is the secret of the show's success?
It's six people with a good sense of humor about things, and that's *always* fun. I know that's what I liked about *Cheers* and *The Mary Tyler Moore Show*. Everyone on the show says something that you're thinking, "That's

what I would say in that situation," except they put it a lot better than you would because they've had nine writers working on it for a few weeks.

Who are all these people watching *Friends*?
It's *amazing* who relates to this show. In New York City I met some very strange and ultra-frightening people who were pierced all over their bodies, and they told me, "You guys are *just* like our friends. We think Ross is *really* cute."

When did you know the show was a phenomenon?
When I started hearing about drinking games on the Internet. They have all these rules like start drinking if Chandler says something funny. And if Barry shows up, drink *everything*.

So have you ever been tempted to play these *Friends* drinking games?
No, I could *never* drink that much.

Do you see *Friends* as having a message?
I don't look at it that way. There's enough stuff in there, you can get out of it whatever you want. And then when you watch it in reruns in five years, you'll probably get something else out of it.

How has the cast avoided ego problems?
We keep one another in check. If I threw a tantrum, I *know* Matthew Perry would be the first one to mock me.

So what was the biggest fight on the set about?
Well, one time there was a row. We were all playing poker and someone wanted to take a cool "Speed Racer" picture down from the wall in the poker room and put it in their dressing room. That's as tense as it's gotten.

So do you see Phoebe as the original riot grrrl?
I *do*. I see an album, tours. I think she's really got something.

MATT LEBLANC

Joey Tribbiani has grown as a man right before our very eyes. Originally meant to be more of a traditional macho stud—remember how he hit on Rachel while she was still in her wedding dress?—Joey has since evolved quite impressively. On the other hand, Joey's abilities as an aspiring thespian may not have improved comparably, although he certainly brought impressive conviction to his lead role in that woefully misunderstood musical *Freud!* And who can blame Tribbiani—or The Artist Formerly Known as Holden McGroin—for wanting more motivation when he served briefly as Al Pacino's butt double. It seems as though Joey first came into the circle of friends by replacing that bum Kip as Chandler's roommate. Last season, Joey briefly screwed up his parents' relationship by encouraging his father to confess to his

mother about a long-term affair. More often than not, Joey's an honorable fellow, and his tremendous sensitivity in "The One with the Birth" suggests that someday he'll make a fine dad.

A far more gifted actor than Joey, Matt LeBlanc went to New York City after high school graduation. Before long he was able to quit his job at Fatburger and make a living doing TV commercials for companies like Levi's and Coca-Cola. From there, he quickly made the transition to TV work in *TV 101, Top of the Heap, Vinnie & Bobbie,* and *Red Shoe Diaries.* LeBlanc—a motorcycle buff and devoted landscape photographer—also appeared in the feature film *Looking Italian.* And though he's often played Italian characters, LeBlanc is actually of mixed heritage—Italian, French, English, Irish, and Dutch. During this past summer hiatus, LeBlanc filmed a starring role in *Ed,* a family baseball movie in which he found himself working with a chimpanzee—this time an animatronic creature.

What do you remember about your *Friends* audition?
There were three Joeys lined up, but they were all different. One was like a blond-haired skinny kind of skateboarder-looking guy. The other was more of a Midwestern-looking guy. And then there was me, the New York Italian-looking guy. The thing is you never really know what people are looking for in those situations.

How would you describe the atmosphere behind the scenes at *Friends*?
Everyone's always knocking on wood hoping that things stay as perfect as they've been so far. Personally, I'm just incredibly thrilled and grateful to be working. Before *Friends* came along, I'd sold my truck, I'd sold my motorcycle, and I'd moved out of the house I was living in to a smaller apartment. Everything was looking pretty damn grim.

Did you feel as though the show's cast got along right from the beginning?
Yeah, that was probably the greatest thing about the whole first season. We all just clicked as actors from day one. And from there I've really grown to care about these people. And I think we all feel the same way.

So you actually do consider the other cast members to be friends now.
Absolutely. On the other hand, I get calls from my other friends and they're all like "Where the hell have you been, man?" These days I barely have time to make sure that I have enough clean underwear in the drawer.

Tell me why a lusty lad like Joey has been so chaste with the female friends.
It's a line you establish that you don't cross. I know I've been in situations like that with my own female friends. I think that when you really cherish the friendship, you know that if you go beyond that line, you may ruin the whole thing. And the truth is that there's something nice about having a woman's point of view on things just as a friend.

How likely would fans be to find you in some groovy coffee-house like Central Perk?
I *never* hang out in coffeehouses. *Never*. To me it's just a metaphor for any gathering place, a socially acceptable place for us all to congregate. A bar's

been done. We were all at a bar one night for Jennifer Aniston's birthday and Jim Burrows—who helped make *Cheers* what it was—came with us. He put his hands on the bar and said, "You know, I think there's a *show* in this."

When people recognize you out in public, what do they want to know?
The most common question I get is "Are you guys *really* good friends?" There are times when I tell them that I don't want to talk about those friggin' people anymore. And sometimes I tell them the truth, which is that we all get along great.

So what kind of fan mail do you and Joey get?
Mostly it's just been requests for photos; then there's the woman who sent Schwimmer her underwear.

Do you have a favorite *Friends* episode?
I really like "The One with the Birth," when Ross' baby is born. There's a great story line, and I was really proud of Joey in that one.

Any theories about why everyone seems to be embracing the show?
I think one reason is that the six of us are so different from one another that everyone relates to one or more of us. Then there's the fact that the show is really good. That helps.

The eminently lovable Chandler Bing is *Friends'* resident wiseass, the uncrowned king of comic self-deprecation. He's the sardonic product of a wildly dysfunctional childhood—he has described his best-selling romance writer mother Nora (a confessed Ross-kisser) as "a Freudian nightmare" and his father as a real gender-bender. Chandler apparently met his pal Ross Geller back in college and later ended up living across the hall from

Ross' fetching little sister Monica. After a rather painful split with his old roommate Kip, Chandler ended up cohabiting happily with Joey Tribbiani, thus forming one of *Friends'* most successful odd couples. Chandler's social life has been less than perfect—though God knows there's always Janice. He's not gay, but supposedly he's got "a quality." The workplace has been the source of considerable frustration for this underachiever who found himself stuck for years at a temporary job in data processing. Fortunately, a big promotion and office upgrade seems to have boosted Chandler's passion for keeping up the corporate WENUS.

Until now, Matthew Perry could certainly relate to some of Chandler's career frustrations—at a young age, he's already been through enough mediocre TV shows to be a grizzled character actor. Remember *Second Chance*, *Boys Will Be Boys*, *Sydney*, or *Home Free*? No, huh? Raised in Ottawa, Ontario, in Canada, where he was at one time a nationally ranked junior tennis player, Perry moved to Los Angeles at age fifteen. There he starting turning up in episodic television (*Beverly Hills 90210*, *Dream On*, *Charles in Charge*, *Growing Pains*) and also appeared in a number of feature films, including 1988's *A Night in the Life of Jimmy Reardon* with River Phoenix and 1989's *She's Out of Control* with Tony Danza. An occasional contributor of gag lines to *Friends* scripts, Perry and his writing partner sold a pilot

called *Maxwell's House*, to Universal
Television. Then happily for all of us, he
signed up to join the *Friends* family, and
the rest has been perfection.

And *yes*, Perry's father John Bennett
Perry really did play the Old Spice guy.

Tell me about your first role.
In seventh grade, I played the fastest gun in
the West in *The Death and Life of Sneaky
Finch*.

I heard you were wonderful.
Oh yes, the notices in the trades were *excellent*.

**How did you land the role in *A Night in the Life of Jimmy
Reardon*?**
I was at a restaurant and I got a note on a napkin from a waitress from a
guy who said he was a director who wanted me to be in his next movie. I
was of course skeptical—I figured this movie was going to be called *On
Golden Blonde* and be shot in the back of a van. Instead it ended up being
my first big-deal job.

**I was one of the unfortunate billions who missed you in *She's
Out of Control*. How were you?**
I played a jerk, so I was really showing my range as an actor. It was not
unlike De Niro gaining all that weight for *Raging Bull*.

**And whom did you play in that Valerie Bertinelli vehicle
Sydney?**
In the pilot I was the guy who hit on her all the time; then later they decided to make me her brother. So then they had to go back and reshoot the
first show so that America didn't go "This is disgusting. This is *wrong*."

**What was your first thought when you read the pilot script for
Friends?**
When I read for Chandler I was like, wow, I can shake hands with this guy.

Initially did the show seem very Generation X-ish to you?
I remember the network's concern was that it not be tagged that way so

that *only* Gen X types watched it. It's not like I have a lot of seventy-year-olds writing to me, but my grandfather watches every week and he loves it. He says his friends do too.

How Chandleresque are you really?
Chandler's a sarcastic guy, dry, funny—a guy who's not comfortable unless he's joking and hiding the emotional stuff that's going on with him. And yeah, I can relate to that a little bit.

Are you surprised to find Chandler viewed as a sex symbol?
Is Chandler being viewed as a sex symbol?

Well, by my wife and some of her friends he is.
Really? God bless 'em.

What would you say the show's really about?
I thought the pitch was about people in their twenties who sit around and say funny things. But that's not really what it is. I asked Marta one day and she said they'd come off working on *Dream On*, which was about someone who'd made his choices in life and was living with them. *Friends* is about people who are in that period when they're on the verge of deciding what the hell they're going to do with their lives.

Has stardom been everything you imagined?
The clichés you hear about—you get on a hit show and get assigned super-models and they beg you to marry them—none of that is happening. There's *no* begging, at least on *their* part. The big change is I get up in the morning and go somewhere I like.

Have you heard from any powerful *Friends* fans?
I haven't heard from Clinton, but Maggie Thatcher's a *big* fan, especially of Chandler and Joey's scenes. She *loves* that stuff.

DAVID SCHWIMMER

For much of the first season of *Friends*, the long-suffering paleontologist Ross Geller seemed a little like TV's very own Job—his torment was biblical. In the pilot, poor Ross had just been left by his beloved wife Carol, who had fallen in love with another woman. By the end of that first episode, he was already carrying a rather large torch for Rachel Green. It turned out that Ross had had a crush on her since the days when she was the high school pal of his little sister Monica. As the season went on, Ross suffered memorably as Rachel somehow remained utterly clueless about the fact that this Übermensch wanted to be more than friends. This sad state of affairs had to be tough to take for this undisputed prince of the Geller clan. What else could the guy do but get a monkey and throw himself into the "bone things" at work. Fortunately, Ross seems to be having somewhat better luck in the second season.

The gifted David Schwimmer himself is the fortunate son of two lawyers. He got hooked on acting while attending Beverly Hills High. A summer program in acting at Chicago's Northwestern University sold him on the place, and he returned there for college, receiving a B.S. in speech/theater in 1988. After graduation, Schwimmer and some of his classmates formed Chicago's acclaimed Lookingglass Theater Company, where he not only acted but also directed various productions. TV beckoned and Schwimmer went on to appear on *NYPD Blue* (as the vigilante nebbish "4B"), *L.A. Law*, *The Wonder Years*, and in a regular role on the failed sitcom *Monty*. He has also been seen in a number of films, including *Wolf*, *Crossing the Bridge*, *Flight of the Intruder*, and *Twenty Bucks*. During *Friends'* summer hiatus, Schwimmer found time for a starring role in *The Pallbearer*, a black comedy with Barbara Hershey and Gwyneth Paltrow.

How difficult is it for the cast to travel in packs now?
When there are two or more of us out there in public, it can get kind of out of hand, which is cool but a little weird. There's definitely a cost-benefit analysis to be made when it comes to being on a successful show. It's great to get all the positive feedback, but the cost is that a private life becomes more and more difficult. I remember when we first went on a trip to Vegas and Jim Burrows said, "Enjoy it, because this is the last time that you are going to hang out all together without a commotion." We were both excited and terrified of that premonition.

Do you miss having the time to do more theater work?
Yes. Believe me, it's a huge and constant conflict.

Did the *Friends* cast start bonding right away?
When you're doing a pilot the reality is that you don't bond too much because any one of you could be yanked at that point. It wasn't until like six episodes that we realized we were all here for good.

Do you find it odd that more of the friends on the show don't sleep together?
No, I have a lot of girlfriends whom I've never been involved with. Those kinds of lines get drawn pretty early on. At the same time, I don't think there's ever a male-female relationship where at least one of the people isn't attracted.

How many months of intensive research on paleontology did you have to do to fully prepare you to play Ross?
At first I actually did some research, and read up on paleontology. Then I realized that the whole subject just never came up.

Still, I get the definite sense that Ross is an excellent paleontologist.
Oh, thank you very much.

After all the rumors of inter-species on-set tensions, what are your feelings toward the monkey?
God bless the monkey.

With all the success of the show, how do you squeeze in your nontelevised friends?

The problem is making time when you seem to have none. The toughest challenge is prioritizing your relationships.

What kind of reaction do you get from people about Carol leaving Ross for another woman?

A couple times I had guys on the street say, "Dude, my friend went through the *same* thing." I have to explain that it's never happened to me and I'm actually not planning on it either.

Is there any sense of competitiveness between the cast members about who gets the most media attention?

That sort of thing can cause tension, but only if you let it. We always talk things out among us.

After other less happy TV experiences, do you feel especially proud of this show?

Unbelievably. I'm really proud of every show that we've done. And what's so empowering about being on this show is that they really respect the actors.

Why do you think it is that *Friends* connects so powerfully with its audience?

I think it's a fantasy family at a time when family unfortunately is so dysfunctional for this generation. The writing's really amazing and the cast has so much chemistry it *reeks*.

FRIENDS PRODUCTION CREDITS

CAST: Jennifer Aniston
       Courteney Cox
       Lisa Kudrow
       Matt LeBlanc
       Matthew Perry
       David Schwimmer

CREATED BY: David Crane & Marta Kauffman

EXECUTIVE PRODUCERS: Kevin S. Bright
                      Marta Kauffman
                      David Crane

SUPERVISING PRODUCER: Michael Borkow

PRODUCERS: Todd Stevens
            Betsy Borns

ASSOCIATE PRODUCERS: Wendy Knoller
                      Mary McLoughlin

CASTING: Barbara Miller
          Leslie Litt

PRODUCTION COMPANY: Bright/Kauffman/Crane
                     Productions, Inc. in association
                     with Warner Bros. Television